D1121852

F*ck
Silence

F*ck
Silence

Calling Trump Out
for the Cultish, Moronic,
Authoritarian Con Man He Is

Joe Walsh

BROADSIDE BOOKS

HarperCollins books may be purchased for educational, business, or sales promotional use. For information, please email the Special Markets Department at SPsales@harpercollins.com.

Broadside Books™ and the Broadside logo are trademarks of HarperCollins Publishers.

FIRST EDITION

Library of Congress Cataloging-in-Publication Data has been ap-plied for.

ISBN 978-0-06-301002-4

20 21 22 23 24   LSC   10 9 8 7 6 5 4 3 2 1

CONTENTS

F*ck
Silence

OPENING MONOLOGUE

L et's get the boring part out of the way first. My name is Joe
Walsh, and I don't own a guitar.

I was elected to Congress from a district in greater Chicago during the Tea Party wave in 2010. I ran as a freedom-
loving, limited-government conservative. I voted like one when
I was in office: against runaway spending and regulations that
screwed over job creators and for lower taxes and free trade
agreements I thought would help Americans through the
toughest economy we faced since the Great Depression. I opposed Obamacare. I supported strong borders. I believed in following what the Constitution told the legislative branch to do
(make the laws) and the executive branch to do (enforce the
laws)—which meant that when a president tried to do Congress's job, it was my duty to stand against him, regardless if
he was a Democrat or a Republican. Those were my positions
when the voters of the Illinois 8th Congressional District chose
someone else to represent them in 2012. They were my positions when I hosted a nationally syndicated radio show between
2013 and 2019. And they are my positions today.

This biographical stuff is usually saved for the jacket cover,

I know. The reason I put it here is that I want you, the reader, to understand where I'm coming from when I make the arguments you're about to read. President Donald Trump and I agree on some big issues. We both believe strongly that illegal immigration threatens our national security and strains our government. He made building a wall on the southern border a focus of his 2016 presidential campaign; I was for a border wall years before that election. He pledged to help unemployed workers in dilapidated manufacturing towns get back onto their feet—the very people who live in my backyard, in places such as Gary, Indiana, and Decatur, Illinois, and who called into my show to talk about an America that wasn't as great for them as it used to be. Trump complained about a political system that was out of touch with ordinary folks, and he promised to get rid of the fancy assholes who ran it.

That was all great. It was part of the reason that I voted for him—for disruption. But that vote wasn't worth it if it means having a president who lies, bullies, abuses his power, places his vanity above the public interest, runs his administration like a cult, manipulates the laws for his personal benefit, befriends dictators while disavowing his own intelligence community, and fails in so many other ways—having nothing to do with being a member of one political party or another—to be a responsible steward of his office. Whether we intended to or not, this package of a little good and a ton of bad is what I and nearly 63 million other Americans voted into office. I believe now that this support was misplaced, and I want to explain to those 63 million why.

I don't believe I can do it by behaving like Trump, and I wouldn't want to, either—by name-calling, mischaracterizing, exaggerating, and pitting people against each other. After all, if I truly believe that Donald Trump is a con man—and I do—

then I myself was conned. I have to own that. But by owning it, I hope to lead others to the same realization—not by making them feel guilty about a politician they backed but by helping them understand the reality of who that politician is, what he's done, and what history suggests he'll continue to do. Sorting through all the information available to us about politics to find the truth of the matter is tough enough already. It's difficult to use that information to help us make knowledgeable choices about our government. So I'd rather try to educate and persuade than lecture and condemn.

What qualifies me to do this? Well, let's start with what I'm not. I'm not a Democrat, so my criticisms aren't just a cover for what I think about Donald Trump's ideology. And I'm not a member of the media, a group that the people in Trump's camp don't trust to provide accurate news, especially about him. Republicans instinctively doubt the fairness of the mainstream press, and believe me, I get it. There are far more Democrats and liberals in newsrooms than there are Republicans and conservatives.[1] That kind of imbalance means there are blind spots or even biases in coverage that disadvantage the Right—even if the majority of journalists are smart people putting in honest work, as I believe they are. But the Trump era has blown the idea of a skewed media out of proportion. This is a president who calls our free press a literal enemy of the people. It's a cop-out to say he means that only for "fake news." Unless you're an outlet dedicated to propagandizing on his behalf, a commentator who arrives at a conclusion he likes, a friendly opinion host on a cable channel, or some internet personality who will fork over your shame, your spine, and your sensibility just for a retweet from @realDonaldTrump, you're "fake news" in the eye of the president. It is every bit that black and white.

What I offer instead is perspective: perspective as someone

who voted for Donald Trump, who understands and has identified with his populist worldview, and who echoed the worst
parts of his divisive and even bigoted rhetoric. In fact, I believe
that I helped create this phenomenon in my own small way. I
went on the radio to fight for the policies and the principles that
I believed in. But oftentimes, during the course of waging this
public fight, I went over the line: engaged in ugly personal attacks and participated in the very demagoguery of serious public policy matters that I call out today. I got caught up in the
conservative media outrage machine—that motley crew of in-
cendiaries for whom no "hot take" is ever scalding enough—to
get listeners and internet "clicks." This rhetoric, which is so
widespread on the Right, partly led to the elevation of a man
like Trump to the White House. He is the worst iteration of
the politics of personal destruction. I want to help clean up the
mess he made and prevent us from making another one like it
ever again. I want to do this not to help me sleep easy at night or
to ingratiate myself with the Left, "Never Trump," or a clique
of any kind, but to do the right thing. Because I have the good
fortune and the opportunity to do it. I believe deep in my gut
and in my head that Donald Trump has betrayed conservatives,
crapped all over the rule of law, and damaged this country. And
because of my background, I hope to be a credible source for
making the argument.

I can envision some of the criticism of this: *Well, thanks for
stating the obvious, Joe, but what are you going to do about it?* First,
it's a mistake to assume that most of the public thinks it's "obvious" that Trump is a threat, a real menace, to the nation. That
especially goes for us conservatives, of course, many of whom
get their news from sources that simply paper over the president's unacceptable conduct. Most of the public don't pay atten-

tion to Trump around the clock—but make no mistake, there are people who need to, because the president of the United States can change the world in an instant. I am not included in "most of the public." I am part of an ecosystem in which reporters and pundits and provocateurs watch the president say something almost in real time, then react to it, determine its significance, and before we know it participate in the cycle all over again. Sometimes these flare-ups "make news" the way ordinary Americans are used to seeing it: one of the president's tweets or comments out of the blue will become a story on a newspaper's website or in print, on the radio, or during a television news broadcast. Sometimes they don't. But these examples come so often and fade so quickly *all the time* that it's easy to forget they ever happened.

Second, it's not always evident that the president's acting out is dangerous or leads to a larger risk. Let's take an example from the last year. Do you remember when Trump displayed a map in the Oval Office of Hurricane Dorian's path that was edited with a Sharpie to make it look as though the storm was expected to strike Alabama? It happened during a string of days in early September 2019 when the president kept insisting that the hurricane was set to hit the state "much harder than anticipated." If you don't remember, I can hardly blame you. If you do, please bear with me—this'll take only a minute. The president made his claim on the morning of September 1.[2] He elaborated on it later that day, saying that Dorian "may get a little piece of a great place: It's called Alabama. And Alabama could even be in for at least some very strong winds and something more than that, it could be. This just came up, unfortunately."[3] But the five most recent forecast tracks, between 5:00 p.m. EDT the previous day and 12 hours later predicted that the hurricane would take a northeasterly path along the Atlantic. The possible extremes for the storm's center stretched east to west from hundreds of miles off the US coast to southeastern Georgia—a long way from Alabama.[4] So maybe he was communicating some outdated information, or maybe he misinterpreted a map; the one he shared on Twitter from the National Hurricane Center the morning of September 1 showed that there was a 5 percent chance of tropical storm-force winds hitting a sliver of southeastern Alabama in the next five days. (I'm being generous here!) In any event, it wasn't anything Trump couldn't fix by saying "My bad" and deferring to the experts. There was no good reason for him to mistakenly alarm the good people of Dothan.

Except one, apparently: to save face. He refused to say he was incorrect, and he refused to be corrected. Instead, he began sharing anything on Twitter he could find to prove he was right: a "spaghetti model" of the storm's possible tracks dated August 28,[5] a map of predicted winds dated August 30,[6] a clip of a CNN meteorologist saying on the evening of August 28 that Dorian's winds could eventually reach Alabama and Mississippi,[7] each of which was outdated by September 1. The Sharpie-marked map should've been just the cherry on top. Except it wasn't! The same day he put the map in front of the news cameras, September 5—by now Dorian was whipping South Carolina and bound for Canada—the White House released a statement attributed to Homeland Security and Counterterrorism Advisor Rear Admiral Peter Brown that read, in part, "The President's comments [on September 1] were based on that morning's Hurricane Dorian briefing, which included the possibility of tropical storm force winds in southeastern Alabama."[8] A day later, the National Oceanic and Atmospheric Administration (NOAA) released this statement: "From

Wednesday, August 28, through Monday, September 2, the information provided by NOAA and the National Hurricane Center to President Trump and the wider public demonstrated that tropical-storm-force winds from Hurricane Dorian could impact Alabama."[9] Of course, those statements weren't unsolicited. Using common sense here, we know that someone had to have asked for them. Believe the *New York Times* or not—and I do—President Trump ordered NOAA to cover for him, and the message was handed down to his acting chief of staff, Mick Mulvaney, who handed it down to the secretary of commerce, Wilbur Ross, who handed it down to NOAA leadership.[10]

Let's put this into words that our Founding Fathers wouldn't have: That's fucking crazy, all right? It's insane. It does not reflect the behavior of a rational human being, much less a stable president and administration. But some people in the corner of political media sympathetic to Trump tried to downplay the saga's significance. One journalist said, "I must spend way too much time reporting [and] with unplugged people because I totally missed the [S]harpie story. Also I don't know what the [S]harpie story is. I don't care to know what the [S]harpie story is."[11] Several Republicans in Congress have often used this same kind of dismissiveness to say they don't pay attention to the president's Twitter feed, as if nothing he posts to it is of significance. ("I have a long-standing policy that I don't comment on tweets," said Senator Ted Cruz in response to reporters' questions about a derogatory comment Trump had made toward several minority congresswomen, which pretty much captures the spirit of this kind of dodge.)[12]

To get down to the questions, then: Why did any of this *really* matter? And should people disown the president just because he threw a days-long fit about his inaccurate assessment of a storm forecast? Look. If you're a Republican, and your choices are to (a) swallow the childish, stubborn behavior of the person on your side of the aisle and get policy you like in exchange for it or (b) bail, risk empowering progressives, and get policy you don't like, I understand how you could choose (a). It's essentially the choice Republicans made in 2016. But what the last three years have revealed is that *that wasn't actually the choice.* It wasn't just about tolerating childish, stubborn behavior. To take it from the top: to justify his untrue statements that Hurricane Dorian was set to hit Alabama "much harder than anticipated" and that it could bring "at least some very strong winds and something more than that," the president of the United States tweeted expired hurricane maps and a TV weather segment with old information, displayed a doctored storm track in front of a press gaggle in his office, and ordered his subordinates, including the head of a major government science agency, to misrepresent scientific data. Now . . .

Let's pretend for a second that this president doesn't have a name or belong to a political party.

Let's pretend instead that he's just an independent guy doing the job. Let's call him "Bob."

Do you trust Bob to do the job of president?

Do you trust him to put your interests before his if he will risk panicking Americans with false information about a natural disaster just so he can have an excuse to argue with the media?

Do you trust him to give you the facts straight—about the effects of his trade policy, about how many new miles of border wall his administration has built, about an investigation into a foreign adversary's meddling in our election—if he'll bully his employees into lying about the *weather*?

Do you trust him to give you the facts if the stakes are even higher, life and death, if already the stakes of a hurricane are exactly that?

Do you trust Bob to perform the basic constitutional functions of his job? To uphold his oath? To "take care that the laws be faithfully executed"?

Or is the reality that you can't trust Bob even with a box of fucking markers?

You're going to read plenty of times throughout these pages that Donald Trump is unfit to be president. I mean it. But what do I mean? I mean he's incapable of telling the truth and he's incapable of putting the nation's interests ahead of his own. We've seen this countless times these past three-plus years—we saw it in his refusal to acknowledge Russian interference in 2016, we saw it in his push to get China and Ukraine to interfere in the 2020 election, and we saw it in this stupid Sharpie story. While our fellow Americans in the Carolinas were getting pounded by a hurricane, all the president of the United States could talk about was how poorly he was being treated by the press. He made the story about *him*. Not the hurricane. All. About. Him. He cared more about salvaging his reputation than he cared about the Americans adversely affected by a natural disaster. This is who he is. It's why he's "unfit."

And it's why this Sharpie business isn't some trivial story. It's not a story about the president having some fun with his foils in the media, sticking it to the libs, or behaving goofy over a nothingburger. It's a story about a deeply unserious leader whose priority is saving his own skin and who will develop new, often unseemly or illegal ways to do it. This priority is at stark odds with his oath of office: "I do solemnly swear that I will faithfully execute the Office of President of the United States." And you know what? *It's okay if none of this is obvious right off the bat.* Remember when I said it would take "only a minute" to lay out the stuff about Trump and Dorian? Whoops. Not that you were keeping count, but it took a couple thousand words. Explaining the full thrust of Trump's conduct—just how long even one example drags on and the bizarre details of it—takes up a lot of time and space.

So much that you could almost write a book about it.

Chapter 1

THE LIES

The doorman of the building where I hosted my radio show was an older, white-haired gentleman who always struck me as a good, interesting, educated guy. And he couldn't *stand* Donald Trump. His reason, more or less: all Trump does is lie. One morning in May a couple of years ago, he was talking to a construction worker when I walked past. "Hey, Joe!" he called out to me. "Boy—you gonna rip into Trump today?" Trump had cooked up a phony scandal that week: that the FBI had planted a secret source inside his election campaign to spy on him. He had also sent a note to North Korean dictator Kim Jong-un, lamenting that he was canceling a planned summit between them. "I felt a wonderful dialogue was building up between you and me, and ultimately, it is only that dialogue that matters," he wrote to Kim. It was so pathetic it read as though he were backing out of a first date. "Someday, I look very much forward to meeting you."

So, sure, I felt there was plenty to "rip" Trump about.

"Yeah, he always makes it interesting," I told the doorman. But then this working-class construction dude chimed in. "I fuckin' *love* him."

The doorman was taken aback. "All Trump does is lie!" he exclaimed.

"Let me ask you a question," the construction worker said. "What politician dudn't lie?"

That says it all, doesn't it? You and I both know that virtually all politicians lie, fudge, or hedge to a degree. It's the nature of the business. Sometimes it's to frame a bit of data or a development that's clearly bad news as if it were good news. That's called spin. Sometimes it's to misrepresent an opponent's position to try winning a debate. That's called campaign season. The Romans did it. The Founding Fathers did it. Hell, I've done it, not that I'm proud of it. Politicians have always told themselves that to achieve a greater good, it's okay once in a while to tell a little lie. If the public ends up better off for it, who cares, right?

But some lies are bigger than others. I'm in my mid-fifties, which means that I lived through the Bill Clinton era. Through Whitewater. Through Paula Jones and Monica Lewinsky. Through perjury and impeachment. It means that I lived through the FBI catching Representative William Jefferson with $90,000 of cash stuffed in his freezer and a federal court convicting Representative James Traficant of ten felony counts of financial crimes. It means that I lived through the Department of Veterans Affairs secretary lying about wait times at VA hospitals during the Obama administration. Through the IRS scandal. Through Anthony Weiner. But to the construction worker's point, those are just the Democrats. Newt Gingrich had to resign from office after failing to do due diligence on a book deal and giving wrong information to the House Ethics Committee. Then there was the Jack Abramoff Native American Lobbying scandal. Scooter Libby and the Valerie Plame affair. My former colleague in the House and fellow member of the Illinois delegation Aaron Schock using taxpayer money to make his office look like the set of *Downton Abbey*. Literally.

Some people, once they've seen enough, become immune to this kind of misconduct, even the kind that ruins reputations or lands people in prison. It's because they're not looking to some politician to be their moral guidepost. That comes from church, from family, or from community in general. The politician is there to be a culture warrior. To stick it to the elites. To fight. So to the many cynics on Trump's side of things, his inability to tell the truth—to a degree that is practically clinical—just blends in with the rest of those bastards in Washington who are never on the up-and-up. Occasionally, the fib is even worth it if it pisses off the right person. That in itself is an awful reflection of what the baby boomer generation of politics has done to our culture, and it should be more than enough to make people like me pause and wonder how and why we haven't done better.

But right now, in the year 2020, the significance of that construction worker's burnout, shared by tens of millions of American voters, is far greater than a chance for public officials to participate in some self-reflection. Let me get something out of the way here: I am not the world's biggest fan of the Clintons. Sure, I'll grant the obvious: Bill and Hillary are smart people. Those who say otherwise are just kidding themselves. But far beyond my disagreements with them on domestic policy, I resent the fact that their political dynasty has created more turmoil than national unity and misled the country on too many occasions. With that said, let's draw a line. On one end is the most honest politician the United States has ever had. An Abraham Lincoln, for example. Or a George Washington. Even a Mitt Romney, because I'm not sure that guy is capable of lying. On the other end you have Donald Trump.

I'd plot the Clintons closer to Trump on that line. But not right next to him. The effect that Trump has had on the truth is so distorting, few people in American public life have ever gotten even *60 percent* of the way to him—not even the man who said, "I did not have sex with that woman." *What politician dudn't lie?* you ask. Hardly any of them. But that doesn't mean we should give President Trump, a person with the world's largest megaphone, a free pass for broadcasting misinformation every. single. day—which is exactly how extreme his BS is. The general public and government bodies working from a shared set of facts—the unvarnished, independently verified truth of a matter—is absolutely essential to a democracy. As you'll read in more detail later, one of the essential ingredients of a dictatorship is its ability to get away with totally fabricating information, over and over, about issues big and small, usually to make it look perfect and like it's incapable of erring even just a bit. I would argue that conservatives, in particular, historically have prided themselves on rejecting this kind of behavior; just look at our country's great conservative jurists, like the late Antonin Scalia, who was allergic to overinterpreting a statute even a smidge, and instead favored the plainest meaning possible of a law. This tradition is a chief reason why I simply can't support Trump—he represents a severe example of what usually would be a deal-breaker for the conservative movement.

Let's revisit a few specific instances and tie their significance together.

MY CROWD SIZE IS BIGGER THAN YOUR CROWD SIZE

There's always that one signature track from the greatest-hits album that sticks out, right? In retrospect, that's what happened with former White House press secretary Sean Spicer adamantly insisting that the attendance during President Trump's inauguration was the biggest ever. (Narrator: It wasn't.) I want to do two things here: one, quote Spicer during the press conference in which he tells reporters that, despite their eyes, there were more people on and around the National Mall for Trump than there had been for his predecessor, Barack Obama; and two, to outline why the *way* Spicer did this—with over-the-top rhetoric, making him sound like an apparatchik—indicated that the United States of America was dealing with the type of person who would prefer to rule a country with exactly one broadcast tower and television station, both owned by you-know-who.

First, here's Spicer in his own words the evening of January 20, 2017, just hours after the inauguration at the US Capitol (I'm italicizing certain words to point them out):

> [P]hotographs of the inaugural proceedings were intentionally framed in a way, in one particular tweet, to minimize the enormous support that had gathered on the National Mall. *This was the first time in our nation's history that floor coverings have been used to protect the grass on the Mall. That had the effect of highlighting any areas where people were not standing, while in years past the grass eliminated this visual.* This was also the first time that fencing and magnetometers went as far back on the Mall, preventing hundreds of thousands of people from

being able to access the Mall as quickly as they had in inaugurations past.

Inaccurate numbers involving crowd size were also tweeted. *No one had numbers, because the National Park Service, which controls the National Mall, does not put any out.* By the way, this applies to any attempts to try to count the number of protestors today in the same fashion.

We do know a few things, so let's go through the facts. We know that from the platform where the President was sworn in, to 4th Street, it holds about 250,000 people. From 4th Street to the media tent is about another 220,000. And from the media tent to the Washington Monument, another 250,000 people. All of this space was full when the President took the Oath of Office. We know that 420,000 people used the D.C. Metro public transit yesterday, which actually compares to 317,000 that used it for President Obama's last inaugural. *This was the largest audience to ever witness an inauguration—period—both in person and around the globe.* Even the *New York Times* printed a photograph showing a misrepresentation of the crowd in the original Tweet in their paper, which showed the full extent of the support, depth in crowd, and intensity that existed.

These attempts to lessen the enthusiasm of the inauguration are shameful and wrong. The President was also at the—*as you know, the President was also at the Central Intelligence Agency and greeted by a raucous overflow crowd of some 400-plus CIA employees.* There were over 1,000 requests to attend, prompting the President to note that he'll have to come back to greet the rest. *The employees were ecstatic that he's the new Commander-in-Chief, and he delivered them a powerful and important message. He told them he has their back, and they were grateful for that. They gave him a five-minute standing ovation at the end in a display of their patriotism and their enthusiasm for his presidency.*[1]

Where to begin? First, from that speech we knew up front that the administration would politicize nonpartisan or independent agencies, even those entrusted with protecting the United States, just to make Trump look good. CIA personnel were "ecstatic that he's the new Commander-in-Chief"? And "they gave him a five-minute standing ovation . . . in a display of . . . their enthusiasm for his presidency"? What, did he have someone look up their voter registrations? Was this a postcampaign rally? It's just gross. I'm going to be hammering on this idea a lot in this book: that is how Big Brother or a king or a dictator behaves; not the president of the United States.

But there'll be more about that cultish behavior later, even if it's worth highlighting whenever we come across it. On the topic of Trump and his team's lying, did you notice the lengths to which Spicer went to prove something he himself admitted he couldn't prove, something that wasn't that big of a deal to begin with? As always, such a vigorous defense didn't just come from the goodness of one of the president's aide's hearts. Prior to the press briefing at the CIA gathering that Spicer described, Trump said:

[W]e had a massive field of people. You saw them. Packed. I get up this morning, I turn on one of the networks, and they show an empty field. I say, wait a minute, I made a speech. I looked out, the field was—it looked like a million, million and a half people. They showed a field where there were practically nobody standing there. And they said, "Donald Trump did not draw well." I said, "It was almost raining, the rain should have scared them away, but God looked down and he said, we're not going to let it rain on your speech." . . . But, you know, we have something that's amazing because we had—it looked, honestly, it looked like a million and a half people. Whatever it was, it was. But it went all the way back to the Washington Monument. And I turn on—and by mistake I get this network, and it showed an empty field. And it said we drew 250,000 people. Now, that's not bad, but it's a lie. We had 250,000 people literally around— you know, in the little bowl that we constructed. That was 250,000 people. The rest of the 20-block area, all the way back to the Washington Monument, was packed. So we caught them, and we caught them in a beauty. And I think they're going to pay a big price.[2]

On and on and on the rambling went—this at Langley, Virginia, in front of the CIA Memorial Wall, which honors CIA employees who have died in the line of duty. So the water Spicer carried was handed to him by his boss. Whereas Trump mentioned TV coverage, Spicer's particular beef was with a side-by-side photograph in the *New York Times* comparing the inaugural crowd in 2017 with the one in 2009,[3] which he called "a misrepresentation."[4] But it wasn't a misrepresentation, since the photographs were taken from the same vantage point (atop the Washington Monument) at roughly the same time eight years apart, and presidential inaugurations occur at the same hour every four years. There simply were more people standing on the National Mall during President Obama's first inauguration than there were during Trump's—a person's eyes don't deceive *that* much. Still, Spicer tried to set the straight record askew. He mentioned that "floor coverings have been used to protect the grass on the Mall," which "had the effect of highlighting any areas where people were not standing"—as if that had anything to do with how many people had been standing in a given area. He mentioned how many people certain sections of the Mall are capable of holding, including "from the media tent to the Washington Monument, [which holds] another 250,000 people. All of this space was full when the President took the Oath of Office," he said.[5] But it wasn't, based on bird's-eye views and reporting from the ground at the time.[6]

"We know that 420,000 people used the D.C. Metro public transit yesterday, which actually compares to 317,000 that used it for President Obama's last inaugural," he said—but the Metro's own numbers, which were public, quoted 193,000, not 420,000.[7] All of those falsehoods to satisfy the ego of a person who clearly has self-image problems.

Again, anyone who doubts or wants to minimize the significance of that spat with the media could say that it distracted from the "real issues" or that it didn't have anything to do with people losing their medical insurance or their jobs. That's true. But those aren't proofs that the episode wasn't important. They're non sequiturs. The Trump administration decided, on its first day, to launch an Orwellian attack against the media, telling the public to believe a narrative backed by lies instead of publicly available information. And the way it did that was by declaring that its competing account was just as legitimate as the factual one.

"Sean Spicer, our press secretary, gave alternative facts," was how White House counselor Kellyanne Conway put it.[8] And that is how the term "alternative facts" was born.

LYING ABOUT POLICY

So you're "the state"—the big, all-powerful government that steers the country one way or another on issues foreign and domestic. Less than twenty-four hours after taking charge of it, you've established that you will support your arguments with "alternative facts": information that you *say* is factual instead of information that *is* factual. You've said, "There's been a lot of talk in the media about the responsibility to hold Donald Trump accountable. . . . it goes two ways. We're going to hold the press accountable, as well."[9] You have placed yourself on an equal footing with mainstream journalism in terms of the ability to discern fact from fiction. You have implied that you are similarly qualified, and similarly credible, to do the job.

Boys and girls, there's no gentle way to say this: That's what dictators do. Full stop. It's not an exaggeration, it's not fearmongering, it's just the way that dictatorial regimes have operated throughout all of human history. You know who peddled "alternative facts"? Josef Stalin did. Mao Zedong did. Guys who weren't in love with the idea of being held accountable for what they said and did by forces outside the control of the state. To avoid that accountability, a dictator has to prevent, eliminate, or at the very least delegitimize anything that could cast doubt on the trustworthiness of his message. And so Sean Spicer was out there on day one saying that "as long as [Trump] serves as the messenger for this incredible movement, he will take his message directly to the American people,"[10] implying that whatever his "message" is, it would be perfect and therefore could be sent straight to the people, bypassing anyone who would check it for accuracy and sanity. Who needs fact checks? (I mean, Trump has tweeted the term "fake news" more than six hundred times as president.[11]) That's a license to lie.

So what do you think Trump does? He lies. Brazenly. He lies about seemingly trivial things, as in his assessment of Hurricane Dorian's threat to Alabama. He lies about things to boost his image, as in saying he won the Electoral College in 2016 in a "landslide"[12] or saying without proof that he "went down to Ground Zero" after 9/11 to help, a claim that he has repeated over the years and no one has ever verified.[13] Because Trump believes he is beyond reproach, of course in his mind Alabama really was under serious threat from that storm, and he really did wipe out Hillary Clinton in the election, and he really was his own kind of hero amid the rubble of the Twin Towers lending a hand to the real heroes who have *fucking died* from breathing poison after trying to save their fellow Americans.

Yeah, some of it is just downright offensive. And yeah, some of it is goofy. Saying that the noise from windmills causes cancer, which he did during a Republican fund-raising dinner last April,[14] may be an absurdity you just can't take literally or seriously or whatever, because this is Donald Trump we're talking about. But just as with the Dorian story, think for a minute what a president could do if he truly believed he had the right to spread untruths with impunity and had convinced the people who worked for him or profited from his presence in office of the same thing.

Seriously, take a few moments to wonder what the "leader of the free world" could do with that kind of authority, that complete lack of restraint.

He could create whatever fictional world he wanted. Not just by taking something or someone maliciously out of context or fabricating something outright—but by doing it over and over and over again until it sounded as though this alternative reality, built on "alternative facts," was the world he truly believed he inhabited. It's the repetition of the lie—the persistent delusion—that makes Trump's behavior unprecedented. As far as the things the media get wrong are concerned, no one can call BS on a fact-checker if the fact-checker is documenting the same example of mendacity for the *one hundredth time*. That may seem like hyperbole, but it's exactly what the *Washington Post*'s fact-checker Glenn Kessler has dealt with since day one of the Trump administration. You may have heard of his "Pinocchio" system: a public figure gets one to four "Pinocchios" depending on the severity of a misleading or wrong remark. The subjectivity of a rating system like that aside, for this president, Kessler began to document "bottomless Pinocchios" for "claims . . . [Trump] has repeated 20 times and were rated as Three or Four Pinocchios by the Fact Checker."[15] Of those statements, Trump has said five of them more than a hundred times.

For example, he has said about two hundred times that the administration is "building the wall," when in fact it's only been able to get money and authority from Congress to put up a bit of new fencing and some replacement barrier for old and obsolete fencing. He's said a similar number of times that the United States "loses" hundreds of billions of dollars via its trade deficits with China and other countries, and it's total BS: saying that one country "loses" money to another in private transactions between their peoples is like saying I "lose" money to Walmart because I buy groceries from it. Is either of these examples particularly pernicious, or are they just the garden-variety overstatements that the construction worker would roll his eyes at? I argue that it's the first one—because Trump's persona is all about misrepresenting facts, and when you couple that with a misunderstanding of a big issue such as trade, you get a person who lies about important things he doesn't even understand. And he happens to be in such an important job that when he lies because he's out of his depth, he comforts or roils markets, shocks other nations, and affects essentially the entire globe in some measurable way.

A man living in a delusion at the very top of the government sets the tone for others on down. Look past Spicer feeding Trump's narcissism; there are other examples that pertain to government policy. Let me preface this by saying that I'm an immigration hawk. I'm for strong borders. And I've never minced my words when talking about the threat of terrorism. But I think there are plenty of sound data out there for me to justify my positions on those matters without misinforming the country with bad numbers.

For instance, President Trump said during his first State of the Union address that "[a]ccording to data provided by the Department of Justice, the vast majority of individuals convicted of terrorism and terrorism-related offenses since 9/11 came here from outside of our country."[16]

DOJ and the Department of Homeland Security released a report the following year, in January 2018, essentially providing the meat for that claim. It said that 402 of the 549 individuals who had been convicted of "international terrorism-related charges" in US federal courts between 9/11 and the end of 2016 were foreign-born.[17] The report was clear, as Trump tweeted: "New report from DOJ & DHS shows that nearly 3 in 4 individuals convicted of terrorism-related charges are foreign-born. We have submitted to Congress a list of resources and reforms. . . . we need to keep America safe, including moving away from a random chain migration and lottery system, to one that is merit-based."[18]

There are a few glaring problems with this, though. One,

the government's data don't say which of those people had been extradited to the United States to stand trial and therefore wouldn't have been affected by immigration policy. Two, the data don't say which individuals actually *did* benefit from particular immigration policies such as "chain migration." And three, the data exclude domestic terrorism, which is sloppy considering how many more convictions there are for it than there are for international terrorism.

Now, if you're a cynic, this may seem like par for the course, as far as caring about the government distorting statistics. But the government itself disagrees with you. The Justice Department eventually admitted that its report "could be criticized by some readers" and "could cause some readers of the report to question its objectivity."[19] The department didn't retract and pull it down, though—which means that the information the government *itself* implies is misleading still forms the backbone of one of the Trump administration's most prominent stances. That's wrong, and it's also a pretty disgusting way to blanketly smear immigrants as risks to our communities' safety.

So here's the pattern: Trump lies when he sleeps. He lies when he wakes. He lies when it snows. He lies when it rains. He lies on a Monday. He lies every Friday. He lies when he eats. He lies when he tweets. He lies standing up, sitting down, and on his back. He lies to you and me. He'll lie again at the count of three. Oftentimes it's so shameless that the lie can be called out just by searching what he himself said on the record or tweeted on an earlier date in the not-too-distant past.

"The Fake News is saying that I am willing to meet with Iran, 'No Conditions.' That is an incorrect statement (as usual!)," he tweeted in September 2019.[20] But Vice President Mike Pence said in June, "The president of the United States has made it clear we're prepared to talk to Iran without preconditions."[21] One of Trump's spokesmen, Hogan Gidley, said a couple of months later in August, "Well, listen, [Trump] has been clear that he wants to have conversations with the leaders of Iran without, you know, preconditions. He's been very clear about that."[22] The week before Trump's tweet, the Treasury secretary, Steven Mnuchin, said, "Now the President has made clear he is happy to take a meeting with no preconditions,"[23] and Secretary of State Mike Pompeo said, "The President has made very clear he is prepared to meet with no preconditions."[24] And, of course, Trump *himself* said he'd meet with the leadership of Iran without preconditions. Twice: once in July 2018, when he said, "No preconditions. No. If they want to meet, I'll meet. Anytime they want. Anytime they want. It's good for the country, good for them, good for us, and good for the world. No preconditions. If they want to meet, I'll meet."; the other time in June 2019, when he said, "You want to talk? Good. Otherwise you can have a bad economy for the next three years. . . . no preconditions."[25]

There's little to add to this. It has nothing to do with Trump being mischaracterized. It has nothing to with "fake news." It's an off-the-charts rewriting of history, and the stakes are no less than negotiating with an adversary that aspires to possess nuclear weapons. *That* is why it matters that Trump is a serial liar—because he will, by definition, lie about anything.

I say this with tough love; anyone who appreciates democracy has to oppose this type of behavior categorically. Our society is complex, and a lot of reasonable answers to the problems it faces probably land somewhere in the gray area. Tolerating or not tolerating the nation's chief executive habitually lying and creating a culture of lying inside the government is firmly a matter of black and white. We must denounce it together. If we don't, we will allow our nation's leaders and their supporters to base the legitimacy of facts on whether or not those facts support their goals. That's a tool that tyrants have always used to justify their actions—and to appreciate the seriousness of this, please do use your imagination.

Donald Trump has the nuclear launch codes. Think about it.

Chapter 2

THE CONSTITUTION BREAKER

D onald Trump has never shown much respect for the rules of any game he's played: politics, real estate, even golf, at which he's a notorious cheat.[1] He doesn't enter a situation and ask what he's permitted to do. He enters and does whatever he feels like doing. Having a complete lack of respect for institutions and their guardrails is about the least traditionally conservative instinct a person can have. But Trump isn't really a conservative. There ain't a core idea in his body. Instead, he's all about "making deals" just to say he did and getting people to think he's a genius for doing so. You generally need at least a handshake in the business world for each piece of work. But not in the world of being president.

The US presidency has become arguably the world's most powerful job, way more powerful than the Framers intended it to be. Some of its powers are inherently yuge, such as being "commander in chief" of the armed forces—which today make up the mightiest military of any nation on Earth. Presidents make treaties. Presidents fill the federal courts. Presidents, by design, are largely responsible for determining the course of the country. But as the government has grown, they've taken even

fuller control of the wheel. They have a lot of latitude to implement vague laws that Congress sends to them, which is partly
how we've ended up with the monstrosity of a bureaucracy that
barely anyone but the people who staff it in greater Washington, DC, like. And presidents have a mystique about them that
other powerful government officers, such as the Speaker of the
House of Representatives, lack.

Trump apparently caught wind of that mystique and has
exploited it for all it's worth. You're kidding yourself if you
think his campaign slogan was genuinely "Make America great
again." It was really "Mirror, mirror, on the wall." This is a
person so in love with control and his own fame that he once
said, "When you're a star, [women] let you do it. You can do
anything: Grab 'em by the pussy, you can do anything." Fourteen years later, in his current job, he said the Constitution has
for him an "Article 2, where I have the right to do whatever I
want as President," including obstructing justice.[2] *When you're a
star, you can do anything; when you're president, you have the right
to do whatever you want.* The line you can draw from that first
quotation to the next is dead straight: a man who thinks the
rules don't apply to him does whatever he wants to do in private life and then does whatever he wants to do in public life
as well. Could it be any easier to spot a person who thinks he's
above the law—including the Constitution of the United States
of America?

The Constitution makes it pretty clear what presidents
can and cannot do. That Article II Trump mentioned: it says
that the president gets a fixed salary during his term, "and he
shall not receive within that Period any other Emolument"—
meaning a salary, fee, or profit from employment or office—
"from the United States, or any of them." It also says that he

has the power to grant pardons "for Offenses against the United States." He has the power to fill cabinet posts created by law, but "by and with the Advice and Consent of the Senate." It's his job to update Congress about the "State of the Union, and recommend to their Consideration such Measures as he shall judge necessary and expedient"—but it's Congress's role to pass those measures if it thinks they're a good idea. (That's in Article I, as well as in *Schoolhouse Rock!*)*

President Trump has gone beyond or abused these powers on so many occasions it'd make your head spin.

He's in violation of the emoluments language every time taxpayer dollars are spent at a Trump-owned property. The president may have resigned his titles in his private businesses, but he hasn't divested himself. So when government officials shell out money at, say, the Trump International Hotel, just a ten-minute drive from the White House, it benefits the Trump Organization—and, by association, Trump the man. The watchdog group Citizens for Responsibility and Ethics in Washington (CREW) researches this in detail and updates its findings periodically. Here's an update from August 2019:

> Trump administration officials are especially loyal patrons of the Trump International Hotel in Washington, D.C. In total, CREW has recorded *193 officials who have visited this single property*. These visits give other hotel patrons—who include lobbyists, corporate executives and foreign officials—an exclusive perk: The chance to

---

*Surely you remember your childhood! "I'm just a bill/Yes, I'm only a bill/And if they vote for me on Capitol Hill/Well, then I'm off to the White House/Where I'll wait in a line/With a lot of other bills/For the president to sign."

mingle with the President and other high-level administration officials. The President's D.C. hotel offers paying customers access to powerful officials as well as patronage that puts money directly in the President's pocket. These are valuable commodities that no other luxury hotel in D.C. can offer its clients.

Many of these visits take place en masse, with Trump administration officials flocking to the hotel for an event or party, giving hotel patrons valuable access to many officials at once. Both former White House Press Secretary Sarah Sanders and former Assistant Secretary for Public Affairs at the U.S. Department of the Treasury Tony Sayegh held going away parties at President Trump's D.C. hotel this year. Sanders' party brought 35 administration officials to the hotel, including Secretary of Energy Rick Perry, Secretary of Commerce Wilbur Ross, and Counselor to the President Kellyanne Conway, among others. (My emphasis.)[3]

Let's jump next to the pardon power. Trump has totally undermined the spirit of this incredible authority: a merciful spirit, not a self-interested one. And he's used it to flout the law entirely. In 2017, Maricopa County, Arizona, sheriff Joe Arpaio was convicted by a federal judge of criminal contempt of court for refusing to comply with an order to stop racially profiling Latinos to try to find illegal immigrants.[4] But Trump pardoned him for that very offense a couple of months later.[5] That right there is going around the judicial system completely. You had a judge say to someone under a court order, "I told you to stop doing this thing that takes away people's constitutional rights, and I'm going to enforce it." Then the president steps in and says,

"No, you're not." The pardon power isn't there to stop courts from enforcing the Constitution. How utterly stupid would it be if it was? And how useless would the courts become?

(Lest anyone mistake Arpaio's crime for an exception to an otherwise sterling character, this is the same guy who entrapped an eighteen-year-old man in a faux assassination plot, threw him into jail for four years, and then had to pay him $1.1 million in taxpayer dollars for wrongful arrest. The department had already had to pay "more than $43 million in lawsuit settlements and expenses to the families of jail abuse victims during Arpaio's tenure as sheriff."[6] He once called his "tent city" jail a "concentration camp."[7])

Then there's the way Trump uses pardons as though they're carrots on a stick. It's next-level abuse of power. Special Counsel Robert Mueller's investigation of Russian interference in the 2016 election documented examples of Trump and his counsel Rudy Giuliani openly discussing the possibility of pardoning his subordinates, all while Trump provided them moral support to resist cooperating with the government. The evidence is a combination of public statements and sworn testimony—hardly Washington hearsay.

First up is Paul Manafort, the Trump presidential campaign's chairman. "With respect to Manafort," Mueller wrote, "there is evidence that the President's actions had the potential to influence Manafort's decision whether to cooperate with the government. The President and his personal counsel made repeated statements suggesting that a pardon was a possibility for Manafort, while also making it clear that the President did not want Manafort to 'flip' and cooperate with the government."[8]

Second is Michael Cohen, Trump's longtime personal lawyer. "After the FBI searched Cohen's home and office in April

2018, the President publicly asserted that Cohen would not 'flip' and privately passed messages of support to him. Cohen also discussed pardons with the President's personal counsel and believed that if he stayed on message, he would get a pardon or the President would do 'something else' to make the investigation end."[9]

It's not as though the Mueller investigation was a one-off example of Trump dangling pardons. In April 2019, three people briefed about a conversation between the president and the person he was about to appoint acting secretary of homeland security, Kevin McAleenan, told the *New York Times* that Trump had urged McAleenan to close the southwest border to migrants and said that he would pardon him if the move landed him in legal trouble.[10] Then there was this humdinger in August, reported by the *Washington Post*:

> President Trump is so eager to complete hundreds of miles of border fence ahead of the 2020 presidential election that he has directed aides to fast-track billions of dollars' worth of construction contracts, aggressively seize private land and disregard environmental rules, according to current and former officials involved with the project.
>
> He also has told worried subordinates that he will pardon them of any potential wrongdoing should they have to break laws to get the barriers built quickly, those officials said.[11]

Again, I know that these are reports from the *Times* and the *Post*, and a lot of the people I hope to convince of Trump's unfitness for office recoil at the very mention of the *Times* and the *Post*. But you have to look at this stuff in the aggregate: what *Trump himself* and his lawyer said about Manafort and Cohen, what the *Times* reported based on information from several sources, what the *Post* reported *five months later* with a similar level of detail. Taken together, it's convincing evidence that Trump believes the pardon power's purpose is to get underlings to break the laws for him. Now, you have to be a fucking moron to think this is how the legal system works. Or a mob boss who happens to be president.

A mob boss type needs lackeys around him to carry out his dirty work. Some of those people he can install himself, such as the people in the presidential office directly underneath him, with no approval process but the one he sets up. But the people who are in charge of the various components of the operation—well, they need the advice and consent of the US Senate, in this case. Don't misunderstand: Trump has surrounded himself with some eminently qualified public servants, who have helped keep the country from going further off track than it already has. I'm thinking of people such as retired marine general Jim Mattis, the former defense secretary whose experience, intelligence, and reason were gigantic benefits to the United States' decision-making on military affairs. Nikki Haley, the former UN ambassador, is another one. Dan Coats, the former director of national intelligence; Gina Haspel, the CIA director: these people are the adults in the room, and the Senate confirmed them—because they're quality public servants and deserved the gigs.

But the number of those adults is shrinking. Mattis, Haley, and Coats were gone well before Trump even finished his first term. In many cases, their departures were about the aides being at odds with the president. People such as Sean Hannity can bark "Deep state!" until their tinfoil hats fall off, but if I'm asked to trust a group of people including Coats, who was our ambassador to Germany and a respected senator, and Haspel, who has more than three decades of intelligence experience, and Haley, who was praised by Republicans and former U.N. ambassador Bill Richardson, a Democrat and once New Mexico's governor; or a group led by Trump, who likes listening to dictators more than his own experts, well, I'm taking the Coats-Haspel-Haley group. No wonder their kind is so difficult to keep around.

Instead of draining the swamp, Trump is responsible for an ongoing brain drain in some of the most important parts of the federal government. And as I said, he prefers it this way. It gives him more opportunities to put dodos whose biggest credentials are flattery and submissiveness into cabinet-level jobs. But the Senate isn't a cinch to approve these kinds of people even if his party controls it. So Trump couldn't do it without circumventing the Senate's "advice and consent role." The way he's done it is by placing temps in the vacant positions indefinitely, which skirts federal law. The Federal Vacancies Reform Act of 1998 (FVRA) was enacted to solve the problem of staffing empty, Senate-confirmable positions in a pinch, when doing it via the normal route—the constitutional one—would take too much time. Of course, the assumption was that the president and the Senate would be on the same page about filling the jobs in due course and in good faith. That's not the case with this president.

Taking advantage of the FVRA is how he made Matthew Whitaker acting attorney general in replacement of Jeff Sessions. A refresher about the circumstances here: Trump all but bullied Sessions out of office because he wouldn't act like Trump's legal bodyguard. In a July 19, 2017, interview with the

New York Times, Trump said, "So Jeff Sessions takes the job [of attorney general], gets into the job, recuses himself [from the Russia investigation]. I then have—which, frankly, I think is very unfair to the president. How do you take a job and then recuse yourself? If he would have recused himself before the job, I would have said, 'Thanks, Jeff, but I can't, you know, I'm not going to take you.' It's extremely unfair, and that's a mild word, to the president."[12] Six days later, he tweeted, "Attorney General Jeff Sessions has taken a VERY weak position on Hillary Clinton crimes (where are E-mails & DNC server) & Intel leakers!"[13] Two days later he was questioning Sessions publicly again: "Why didn't A.G. Sessions replace Acting FBI Director Andrew McCabe, a Comey friend who was in charge of Clinton investigation but got. . . . . . . big dollars ($700,000) for his wife's political run from Hillary Clinton and her representatives. Drain the Swamp!"[14] The full background of this browbeating aside, the attorney general leads the Department of Justice, which is an *independent law enforcement agency*, not the president's own legal arm, which is the White House counsel. DOJ has historically operated and is supposed to operate without White House influence—much less the president calling the attorney general all but a flimsy dipshit in public. The bullying went on *for another sixteen months* before Sessions finally gave in and quit at Trump's request.

In his place, the White House announced, would be Whitaker—a man who, in private life, had publicly opposed the Mueller probe, had been a Trump mouthpiece on TV during the summer of 2017, and had been appointed Sessions's chief of staff (a position not requiring Senate confirmation) in September of that year. He was elevated from that role to AG when Sessions left office—with the justification of the FVRA.

The law permits the "first assistant" to an official, whatever that means, to fill the previous officer's job if the officer has left because of death, resignation, or vague circumstances that didn't allow the officer to fulfill his or her responsibilities—but not firing. Another key point here: this applies even if the "first assistant" wasn't confirmed by the Senate, like Whitaker. So Trump promoted Whitaker by evading Congress under questionable circumstances, since Sessions's removal was one of those "he said, he said" situations: the official said he had resigned, but the employer said he had been canned. A lot of smart people disagreed about the legality of Whitaker's appointment. But the upshot is that by using a well-intended law that was ripe for abuse, the administration staffed one of the most important roles in the federal government with a flunky that the Senate was unlikely to confirm. You can't trust Donald Trump to do the upstanding thing and not abuse the law.

Whitaker moved on, and after three-plus months Trump replaced him with William Barr, the current attorney general. But that pesky FVRA is still there, and it hasn't been reformed. So Trump has also used it to make Ken Cuccinelli, the former attorney general of Virginia and another fierce Trump defender on cable news panels, the acting director of U.S. Citizenship and Immigration Services (USCIS), the agency tasked with overseeing citizenship, visas, and—somewhat of relevance these days—asylum applications. The way Trump pulled it off was even crazier than the way he had swung it with Whitaker. Cuccinelli met none of the FVRA criteria to fill a Senate-confirmable position; he wasn't even an employee of the executive branch prior to being appointed. So what the Trump administration did was make him "principal deputy director" of USCIS, a position that hadn't previously existed. Because that newly created position was next in line to director and the directorship was vacant, the argument was that the FVRA allowed Cuccinelli to fill the top position. "Seems legit," as they say. Cuccinelli's road to Senate confirmation, like Whitaker's, was likely impassable at the time he was selected. As Senator John Cornyn, the number two Republican in the Senate, put it, "He's made a career of attacking other Republicans and frankly attacking President Trump, so I doubt he'll have the support to get confirmed."[15] A reminder: Cornyn's in the majority. That wouldn't be a case of "Democratic obstruction."

Now, most cheating card players don't announce to the table that they're stacking the deck. That's obvious, right? Well, Donald Trump is an epic dumbass. He's a person with so little knowledge of government process and appreciation for doing things the way they're supposed to be done that he practically stood up and shouted during an interview with CBS, "I'm slipping myself an ace every time, you suckers!" Here's a partial transcript from July 2019 with *Face the Nation*'s Margaret Brennan:

Margaret Brennan: You've had a lot of change-up in your administration recently too. . . . An acting chief of staff. An acting interior secretary.
President Donald Trump: It's OK. *It's easier to make moves when they're acting.*
Margaret Brennan: So you are going to shake up—
President Donald Trump: Some, and some not.
Margaret Brennan: —positions.
President Donald Trump: Some are doing a fantastic job. Really—*I like acting because I can move so quickly.* (My emphasis.)[16]

Really, I like acting because I can move so quickly. I mean, it's so helpful, to ignore the Constitution. An overrated document, really. That's what people are saying.

What an *idiot*.

Trump acts as though he's above Congress in other ways, too. Take its role of making laws. This particular sin is one that has usually struck a nerve with conservatives. Probably the most notorious example to people of my ilk was when President Obama said, "We're not just going to be waiting for legislation in order to make sure that we're providing Americans the kind of help they need. I've got a pen, and I've got a phone." Meaning that if he didn't get a bill he wanted from Congress, he'd just sign an executive action that got his wishes part of the way—or even all of the way—there. I remember when that kind of talk pissed Republicans like me off. Take Mick Mulvaney, a fellow Tea Party rep who was elected to Congress the same year I was. Mulvaney thought we were unfairly maligned for opposing Obama when he said things such as his "pen and phone" comment—and then did things such as creating the Deferred Action for Childhood Arrivals program (DACA) from whole cloth. "When we do it against a Republican president [instead], maybe people will see it was a principled objection in the first place," Mulvaney told then–*National Review* reporter Tim Alberta in 2016.[17]

But Mulvaney, now Trump's acting chief of staff, is not doing it against a Republican president. Instead he's aiding and abetting a Republican president who is overstepping his bounds. And too many Republicans in Congress are sitting idly by.

A substantial piece of evidence comes from early in 2019, when Trump declared a national emergency on the southern border. He made the declaration so he could get funds for the border wall he had promised during the 2016 campaign. There's just one problem: Congress had already decided not to give him the money. That's its prerogative, and the Constitution says so. Congress had funded a few rounds of fencing largely to replace existing, subpar barrier, but it had not doled out cash for a whole, brand-new wall. It's not as though Congress hadn't debated whether it should—it had. Repeatedly. It had taken votes. And up to the moment Trump announced the emergency, it had voted against his wishes. That's how it goes sometimes; that's how the system works. But to restate: Trump does not appreciate the system if it doesn't benefit him. It's not that he's frustrated by it and airs his grievances, which, I dunno, pretty much every chief executive who has had to deal with a legislature has ever done. There's nothing wrong with that. Bitching and moaning? It's all part of the "war of ideas," a consequence of ensuring that the people's representatives have a say in how their constituents' tax dollars are spent. It's what a government looks like when there isn't one-man rule. When there is, a government looks like this: Trump says there's an emergency—that emergency being that *Congress didn't do what I wanted it to do*—then takes money that Congress had appropriated for one purpose and uses it for a different purpose that Congress had rejected. That is the case here.

Trump says he gets this power from the National Emergencies Act (NEA), a statute from the 1970s that laid out a process for presidents to declare emergencies and Congress to regulate them. There hadn't been such a definition in law before; there is no specific presidential "emergency power" in the Constitution, and for almost two centuries, Congress and several presidents (including Lincoln and Franklin D. Roosevelt) just winged it. So the need for something like the NEA was pretty indisputable. But presidents shouldn't be able to manipulate it for something that isn't, by definition, an emergency. An emergency, by definition, occurs suddenly. It demands immediate action. But the very language in Trump's declaration implies that neither of these things was the case on the border. "The problem of large-scale unlawful migration through the southern border is *long-standing*," the declaration reads, "and despite the executive branch's exercise of existing statutory authorities, the situation *has worsened in certain respects in recent years*." (My emphasis.)[18] A "long-standing" problem that has deteriorated over a course of "years" is a complaint about a trend, not a point in time. Forget about a wall. A wall will take years to build, which doesn't address the circumstances of an "emergency." If what was going on in California and Texas was really an emergency, Trump would've sent tens of thousands of troops to the border immediately. Instead, he opted for a cowardly con job to deceive his voters into thinking that he's really, really fighting for a campaign promise. Recall that bit about his reassuring federal officials that he'd pardon them if they broke the law to build the wall: "President Trump is so eager to complete hundreds of miles of border fence ahead of the 2020 presidential election that he has directed aides to fast-track billions of dollars' worth of construction contracts, aggressively seize private land and disregard environmental rules."[19] Trump's various disregards for the law fit together like a flowchart: fill a vacancy illegally with a lackey, reassure the lackey that he'll pardon him if he breaks the law, and go around Congress both times.

No man is above the law, including the president. He isn't above the Constitution. And as of this writing, the one part of Article II he doesn't like to talk about is coming back to bite him. It reads, "The President, Vice President and all civil Officers of the United States, shall be removed from Office on Impeachment for, and Conviction of, Treason, Bribery, or other high Crimes and Misdemeanors."

If you ask me—if you read the words in this chapter and elsewhere in the book—he's guilty.

Chapter 3

THE CONSTITUTION BREAKER, PART TWO

L et's hit "pause" for a minute. Though people of my ideology are fond of talking about the United States' founding documents and the men who wrote them, I'm not trying to imitate a lecture in constitutional law here. It's not my background, and it's not my style. But it is helpful and necessary to describe, just a bit, what parts of our Constitution the president has treated as optional—like a sometimes-but-not-all-the-time sort of arrangement. The previous chapter tells only part of the story of how Trump has broken his presidential oath, which reads, "I do solemnly swear that I will . . . to the best of my ability, preserve, protect and defend the Constitution of the United States." That goes for *all* of it. It goes for Article II, which describes the scope of the presidency. And it goes for the First Amendment, one of the most consequential sets of guarantees and protections for private citizens against a government ever written into law the world over. Putting it here for reference:

Congress shall make no law respecting an establishment of religion, or prohibiting the free exercise thereof; or abridging the freedom of speech, or of the press; or the right of the people peaceably to assemble, and to petition the Government for a redress of grievances.

Even though Trump himself is not "Congress" and he's technically not "making laws" to shut down the First Amendment, this language applies directly to him. It's been settled by the courts that the First Amendment prohibits public officials in general from using government power to retaliate against individuals for their speech.[1] And Trump is the most powerful public official in the nation.

So the question is: Is he fulfilling his responsibility to uphold the First Amendment? Let's see, uhh . . . he's tweeted "fake news" more than six hundred times and said it out loud who knows how many hundreds of times more; he's called the media the "enemy of the people" at least a few dozen times; he's obsessed with "opening up" libel laws; he wants to place speech regulations on social media companies; he unconstitutionally "blocks" people whose speech he doesn't like from seeing the words he posts to those very same social media platforms; his White House suspends the access of reporters whose coverage the administration finds negative; he encourages Americans to boycott businesses affiliated with media companies he despises; he . . . yeah, it doesn't really seem as though he cares about the First Amendment. The rap sheet is pretty long.[2]

Before we get into the details of it, though, let's frame this by showing just how Trump doesn't *understand* First Amendment rights. He tramples over them, sure, but that's because of his complete ignorance. Take his views about freedom of the press, which he articulated during a White House forum in July 2019 featuring—ironically—fringy internet trolls who routinely spread false info.[3] He said, "See, *I don't think that the mainstream media is free speech* either because it's so crooked. It's so dishonest. So, to me, free speech is not when you see something good and then you purposely write bad. To me, that's very dangerous speech, and you become angry at it. But that's not free speech." (My emphasis.)[4] It's rarely easy to interpret Trump's train of thought. But the statement "I don't think that the mainstream media is free speech" is clearer than Casper the Friendly Fucking Ghost.

It's every bit this simple: If, in his opinion, your speech is favorable to him, it's "free speech." If, in his opinion, your speech is unfavorable to him, then it's not protected by law: either it warrants legal action or it falls outside the rights guarded by the Constitution. Read those two sentences again and again and again and again, until that little voice in your head whispers, "Well, that sounds an awful lot like Mao. That sounds an awful lot like Vladimir Putin." You see, in America—my America, your America, and, as much as he may not like it, Donald Trump's America—people can say things and reporters can report things that completely piss us off, and it's their constitutionally protected right to do it. There are exceptions, of course, such as for defamation. But ask yourself: How many times has Trump or his administration called a news story "fake" and followed up even by *trying* to prove it? How many times have they presented evidence to support their claims? How many times have they actually argued that a media organization met the legal standard for defaming a "public figure" like Trump: in the words of Supreme Court justice William Brennan in the 1964 case *New York Times Co. v. Sullivan*, "that the statement was made with knowledge of its falsity or with reckless disregard of whether it was true or false"? If you guessed "virtually zero," "virtually zero," and "absolutely zero," you've won today's prize.

I wrote this earlier and I'll write it again: I get that the media have biases against the Right. I get that they often frame political stories in a way that's unfair to conservatives; that when Alexandria Ocasio-Cortez botches the rollout of a far-reaching, controversial environmental agenda, the story is really that "Ocasio-Cortez Team Flubs a Green New Deal Summary, and Republicans Pounce," and that when the press turns its attention to gun control, it often fails to report accurately about firearms. We absolutely ought to call out these lapses when we notice them—and the Left ought to have a field day with Fox News! There's nothing wrong with either side of this sort of pushback. But Trump has taken something reasonable like attentiveness to fairness in the media and turned it into the basest, most dangerous rallying cry: "the enemy of the people" bullshit. That sort of overreaction is light-years from bias.

Believe it or not, there's a more appropriate—and arguably effective!—way for conservatives to go about setting the press straight. Indeed, it's possible to back up accusations of incorrect reporting. For example, I remember "Rathergate," when CBS almost sank President George W. Bush's reelection campaign with a story about allegedly incriminating National Guard documents that the network utterly failed to verify.[5] That moment in 2004 was a watershed for right-wing internet media— because they helped expose CBS's negligent reporting[6] and force the termination of several people at the network. They sensed wrongdoing—but then they put in the work and got a result. Team Trump doesn't present those kinds of cases, maybe because they're so rare. Here's what digs at Trump so deeply:

journalists typically bust their asses to make sure their stories about him are well sourced and filled with facts, and because they do their due diligence and their reports don't make him look so great a lot of the time, Trump doesn't have the goods to say they're working in bad faith, much less truly breaking the law. All he has is a pathetic cry that he makes over and over: "Fake news! Fake news!" Each tweet drips with tears.

Well, Joe, there's nothing illegal about the president saying "Fake news!" all he wants, so what's the big deal? you may ask. That's an essential question to thinking about this issue. After all, Nixon's vice president, Spiro Agnew, called the media "nattering nabobs of negativism," and no one said he should be given a trial date for it. (That came for other things.) First, I'd say that a relentless campaign to undermine our country's free press—which we absolutely need to hold powerful people and institutions accountable—is bad regardless of the legality of it. It's reckless, it resembles the behavior of a strongman more than a president, and it has the side effect of creating a culture in which people think the First Amendment is there to protect only their tribe, not their political rivals. (More on that later.) But second, bellyaching about "fake news" is only the tip of the iceberg, especially when it happens on average—literally—every other day.* How do you think someone of that perspective, with that amount of fixation, that level of power, and that indifference to being held accountable, acts when he isn't tweeting? "Fake news" is smoke, and the fire's somewhere close by. Look to history as a guide, as this First Amendment lawsuit against Trump does: "The Nixon Administration was

---

*By Trump's one thousandth day in office, he had tweeted the term "fake news" well over five hundred times and said it who knows how often in other forums.

particularly antagonistic to the press and subjected those on an 'enemies list' to illegal wiretaps, tax audits, and office searches. It threatened to take action against broadcast licenses owned by the *Washington Post* in retaliation for its coverage of the Watergate scandal, proposed an official monitoring system through the FCC [Federal Communications Commission], and manipulated tax and antitrust enforcement efforts to punish the press,"[7] the complaint reads. You see, rarely is talk just "talk" when it comes from a regime that acts as though it's above the law. If the president says the media are an enemy, the chances are that he acts on it. That was the case with Nixon—and now it's the case with Trump.

EXAMPLE ONE: BARRING THE MEDIA

The key test of defending the First Amendment is doing it for the people you disagree with. That's the case for me with CNN White House correspondent Jim Acosta and *Washington Post* columnist Dana Milbank.

Acosta's Q-and-A exchanges with President Trump are often infamous. He's become a celebrity journalist, the type of reporter who traffics attention (1.34 million Twitter followers!) and winds up on late-night TV, all because of his combativeness with a White House that—granted—invites it. In November 2018, he made a fool of himself during a press conference, refusing to pass the microphone to other journalists in the room long after Trump had moved on from him. The whole episode was a fiasco—so much so that the president stepped away from the podium to collect himself before pointing at Acosta and saying, "I'll tell you what, CNN should be ashamed of itself, having you working for them. You are a rude, terrible person." It was a bad moment for the press. It was a bad moment for Trump, too, who should be above embarrassing a journalist in front of his colleagues. There were no winners. But look— media combat is the norm for this White House, and no one would've been the lesser if both parties had just moved on from the confrontation.

Of course, Trump—for whom no slight is ever too small— couldn't let it go. Instead, the administration revoked Acosta's White House press credentials. The way it justified doing so was blood boiling: White House press secretary Sarah Hucka- bee Sanders promoted a deceptively edited video of the Trump- Acosta exchange that made it seem as though Acosta had pushed away a White House intern who was trying to seize the mic from him. The source of the video made it all the more in- furiating: it had been created by a contributor to InfoWars, the batshit-crazy, alt-right, alt-reality, conspiracy-theorizing web- site run by lunatic Alex Jones.[8]

Milbank's circumstances weren't nearly as zany. He didn't have a heated encounter with a White House official or any- thing. He just checked his email one day in May 2019, and as he wrote, he saw a message "informing me that Trump's press office had revoked my White House credential." He continued:

> I'm not the only one. I was part of a mass purge of "hard pass" holders after the White House implemented a new standard that designated as unqualified almost the entire White House press corps, including all seven of The Post's White House correspondents. White House officials then chose which journalists would be granted "exceptions." It did this over objections from news or-

ganizations and the White House Correspondents' Association.

The Post requested exceptions for its seven White House reporters and for me, saying that this access is essential to our work (in my case, I often write "sketches" describing the White House scene). The White House press office granted exceptions to the other seven, but not to me. I strongly suspect it's because I'm a Trump critic. The move is perfectly in line with Trump's banning of certain news organizations, including The Post, from his campaign events and his threats to revoke White House credentials of journalists he doesn't like.[9]

Those "threats" were in reference to Trump's comment that "It could be others also" in the press who have their credentials revoked in response to being challenged in ways the administration won't tolerate.[10]

Milbank added this: "[T]here's something wrong with a president having the power to decide which journalists can cover him."[11] That's exactly right. In fact, I'll do him one more: it's absolute bullshit that a president could exercise this kind of power. Taking away the press passes of journalists Trump doesn't like is chilling. It's an attack on the free press. It's the stuff of dictators. And it should be opposed by everyone, including Americans who support Trump's government policies.

I don't have to like Acosta's approach to his work or Milbank's takes on politics to think that the White House's blocking their access to power is unacceptable. For one, if Trump thinks he's a big, bad bully and he wants his administration to project an image of big, bad bullies, then by God he should be able to withstand criticism by Jim stinking Acosta or a withering column by the likes of Milbank. This president is no student of history, but you think at one point he would've heard the saying, "Speak softly and carry a big stick." Teddy Roosevelt did not include at the end of that quote, "and swing it at whoever you can, whenever you can." But the way I'm protesting the administration's retribution here is all about what I think of its weenie-ass attitude. The far more important argument against it is rooted in the Constitution. And so far, the federal courts have borne that argument out. A judge ordered Acosta's press pass temporarily restored less than ten days after the White House took it away.[12] The administration then backed off and permitted Acosta to resume his normal work. Milbank is a member of PEN American Center, the nonprofit advocacy group for writing professionals that filed a First Amendment suit against Trump in US district court.

Of course, I made a point of highlighting these two members of the DC press as individuals I disagree with for one reason or another—and whose rights are just the same as those of the people I do agree with. But other reporters are facing and fighting this same crackdown, too. One of them is Brian Karem, *Playboy*'s White House correspondent (yes, it has one), whose press credentials were revoked last year after he had a brief spat with one of Trump's sycophants in the Rose Garden.[13] Less than two months later, a judge reversed the White House's decision.[14] If you're seeing the makings of a pattern, it's not just you—courts are finding that the Trump administration's retaliation against journalists is against the law. And just so no one thinks that this is another case of "activist" judges, well . . . the judge in Acosta's case was appointed by President Obama, and the judge in Karem's case was appointed by no one other than Donald J. Trump.

EXAMPLE TWO: BOYCOTTING CNN

Trump's clashes with Acosta are indicative of a problem he has with CNN in general. On his fifth day in office, he congratulated Fox News for being a TV ratings monster and noted that its inauguration ratings had been "many times higher than FAKE NEWS @CNN."[15] He's called the network "#FraudNewsCNN," too,[16] suggested that its slogan should be "CNN, THE LEAST TRUSTED NAME IN NEWS,"[17] and concluded that it's "dead."[18] He occasionally retweets images or videos created by Trump fanboys that depict the CNN logo in some violent state, such as a picture showing him seated with his legs crossed and "CNN" in the middle of a blood spatter on the bottom of his shoe.[19] It's pathologic, unhealthy behavior, and I'll take this moment to plug the website http://www.trumptwitterarchive.com, which organizes Trump's tweets by keyword; Americans should visit it to learn more about how much of an unpresidential whack job he is. (There's no avoiding it. It's in the public eye.)

As far as a public official's antagonism toward a news outlet is just a matter of personal preference, it's no big deal. All politicians have that kind of skepticism. I'm a Tea Party–era conservative: I know well that the *New York Times* has a leftist bias and that MSNBC despises Trump. I think CNN leans left but does a pretty good job of playing it fair and balanced with its actual reporting, as opposed to its commentary. These perspectives can affect how much I pay attention to those sources and how reliable I feel they are when I do. It's fine for any public figure to make these sorts of judgments—from Democrats who loathe Fox News to Trump himself. But Trump's open hostility toward CNN, in particular, is potentially dangerous—don't tell me that a cult figure like him promoting a video of a train "hitting" the CNN logo[20] or another one of him "punching" the logo[21] is harmless, when it fits broader patterns of his declaring journalists "enemies" even as journalists the world over are subjected to violent threats and even death.[22] We just can't be that naive or dismissive. Even beyond the way this shameful conduct poisons our society, it's a sign that Trump could be open to more purposeful action than only rhetoric. Sure enough, the president isn't engaged only in a war of words with Jim Acosta and his employer but in a war of actions with potential consequences for the network. *This* specific war is one-sided: Trump's the president, a position with unique cultural influence and government authority, and CNN is a private entity, albeit a large one.

He's used that influence and authority to not-so-subtly call for a boycott of the network's parent company, to force editorial "changes" at the news channel. He tweeted in June 2019, "I believe that if people stoped [*sic*] using or subscribing to @ATT, they would be forced to make big changes at @CNN, which is dying in the ratings anyway. It is so unfair with such bad, Fake News! Why wouldn't they act. When the World watches @CNN, it gets a false picture of USA. Sad!"[23] This is extraordinary on its face. Strip the names of the businesses from the tweet, and think about what it says: it's the chief officer of the federal government using his perch to bully a business he disfavors and threaten it with financial harm. Remember earlier in the book when I quoted Sean Spicer on inauguration day? "There's been a lot of talk in the media about the responsibility to hold Donald Trump accountable. And I'm here to tell you that it goes two ways," he said.[24] Can't say he didn't warn us.

As galling as Trump's boycott suggestion was, there's evidence that he may have been even more intentional in using his official powers as president against CNN. Late in the 2016 campaign, Trump pledged that his Department of Justice would reject a proposed merger between Time Warner—CNN's old owner—and AT&T. He even pointed out the Time Warner–CNN relationship when he made his statement: "As an example of the power structure I'm fighting, AT&T is buying Time Warner and thus CNN, a deal we will not approve in my administration because it's too much concentration of power in the hands of too few."[25] Committing to do something like that is inappropriate. DOJ has approval power over corporate mergers, and its decisions in cases such as Time Warner–AT&T should be based on the facts and its own legal judgment alone. That's because it's an independent law enforcement agency—not the president's personal law firm.

Since Trump had so obviously tipped his hand during the campaign, it was worth keeping track of how the new administration would approach the merger. In November 2017, the Justice Department did file a lawsuit against it.[26] And although the administration's legal challenge failed and the merger was ultimately allowed to go through, what happened in the roughly year and a half in between is of some note. Here's one significant record, via Jane Mayer of *The New Yorker*:

> Although Presidents have traditionally avoided expressing opinions about legal matters pending before the judicial branch, Trump has bluntly criticized the plan. The day after the Justice Department filed suit to stop it, he declared the proposed merger "not good for the country." Trump also claimed that he was "not going to get

involved," and the Justice Department has repeatedly assured the public that he hasn't done so.

However, in the late summer of 2017, a few months before the Justice Department filed suit, Trump ordered Gary Cohn, then the director of the National Economic Council, to pressure the Justice Department to intervene. According to a well-informed source, Trump called Cohn into the Oval Office along with John Kelly, who had just become the chief of staff, and said in exasperation to Kelly, "I've been telling Cohn to get this lawsuit filed and nothing's happened! I've mentioned it fifty times. And nothing's happened. I want to make sure it's filed. I want that deal blocked!"

. . . According to the source, as Cohn walked out of the meeting he told Kelly, "Don't you fucking dare call the Justice Department. We are not going to do business that way."[27]

So did it happen? Mayer added that Cohn declined to comment, Kelly didn't respond to inquiries, and a former White House official "confirmed that Trump often 'vented' in 'frustration' about wanting to block the A.T.&T.–Time Warner merger," not understanding "the nuances of antitrust law or policy."[28] The House Judiciary Committee wanted to learn more, so in March 2019 it asked the White House to turn over records related to the merger. The White House denied the request.[29] So what we're left with is a lot of smoke, no hard proof of fire, and a lot of fair questions about a president who just doesn't appreciate the importance of law enforcement being free of political interference. Oh, and an ongoing war against CNN: as Reuters reported on October 18, 2019, "Lawyers for

U.S. President Donald Trump and his re-election campaign have threatened in a letter to sue CNN for what they said was the network falsely advertising itself as a news organization, calling on executives to first discuss an 'appropriate resolution' to the matter that would include a 'substantial' payment to cover damages."[30]

EXAMPLE THREE: REGULATING SPEECH IN SILICON VALLEY

Now, here's something funny. The same Donald Trump who thinks it's okay for *him* to crack down on speech he doesn't like—by shutting off press access to his administration and directly attacking news organizations with words and official acts—doesn't think it's okay for social media companies to crack down on speech that *they* don't want on *their* platforms. He and many of his allies in right-wing, digital-based media have complained that Trump-sympathetic users have been kicked off the likes of Facebook and Twitter in an illegal display of political prejudice. "Twitter should let the banned Conservative Voices back onto their platform, without restriction. It's called Freedom of Speech, remember," he tweeted in June 2019.[31]

By that date, here are some "Conservative Voices" that Twitter had removed in the previous year-plus: former Milwaukee County sheriff David Clarke, whose account was temporarily suspended after he tweeted, "When LYING LIB MEDIA makes up FAKE NEWS to smear me, the ANTIDOTE is to go right at them. . . . Punch them in the nose & MAKE THEM TASTE THEIR OWN BLOOD";[32] Alex Jones, whose personal account and InfoWars account were taken down permanently after repeated violations of Twitter's terms of use;

Gavin McInnes, the founder of the violent alt-right group Proud Boys, whose own account and those of other Proud Boys were banned "for violating our policy prohibiting violent extremist groups," a Twitter spokesperson said;[33] the actor James Woods, who was locked out of his account for a time after creating an election-related hoax that Twitter identified as violating its terms of service;[34] the far-right activist Laura Loomer, who said her account was suspended after posting a tweet about Representative Ilhan Omar in violation of Twitter's hateful-conduct policy;[35] and Jacob Wohl, the infamous conspiracy theorist and hoaxer whose flattery of Trump is so absurd that I could only describe it with R-rated adjectives.[36]

These are some unsavory characters—wackos, morons, and instigators all. In Twitter's view, they don't belong on its platform. While I don't necessarily agree—my view of free speech is pretty expansive and my tolerance for speech I find deplorable is pretty high—I don't believe that Twitter's judgment and the way it acted on that judgment is illegal. Here's why: *This is a case of private individuals using a private media company as their forum. It's not a case of public officials denying individual speech in some public space.*

This is what Trump and his people don't get about the First Amendment; in fact, it's what they get entirely backward about it. The First Amendment applies to the government—not a social media platform. The First Amendment's language does not read, "No institution, public or private, shall abridge a person's speech." If it did, you know what else arguably could be illegal besides banning idiots from Twitter? A newspaper rejecting an op-ed submission. A company spokesperson shutting down a press conference. "But I have a right to be heard!" the op-ed writer or the reporter shouting a question would say—and by this new stupid definition of "free speech," they'd have a claim. But in the real world, they have no case. The op-ed writer may have been turned down, but (1) it's not because the government told the newspaper not to publish him, (2) the government didn't deny his ability to write or try to get his voice published in the newspaper, (3) he can take his submission to as many different newspapers as he wants, and—this is the big one—(4) there isn't anything in law that says a newspaper has to publish him. So I ask my fellow conservatives who think Twitter has an obligation to allow the likes of InfoWars to publish on its website: Since when did we start believing that the Constitution's purpose was to force others to do what we want them to do? Isn't that the kind of nanny-statism we've denounced all our lives? Or has the equation changed because Trump is our nanny and we want him to fill our bottles with liberal tears?

As of summer 2019, the Trump administration was considering an executive order that would require the FCC "to develop new regulations clarifying how and when the law protects social media websites when they decide to remove or suppress content on their platforms," CNN reported, based on a summary of the order its reporter had seen with his own eyes.[37] The reason, according to a White House official: "If the Internet is going to be presented as this egalitarian platform and most of Twitter is liberal cesspools of venom, then at least the president wants some fairness in the system."[38] Nah, pal. That's weak. The internet and Twitter aren't the same thing. Twitter is like 0.0000000000 . . . 1 percent of the internet. If Twitter doesn't like your shtick, then take it somewhere else. And if "somewhere else" doesn't like it, either, consider the possibility that in the marketplace of ideas, your ideas suck.

THE ANTI—FIRST AMENDMENT CULTURE

It's straightforward:

- One, yes, Facebook, Twitter, and YouTube all have a left-of-center bias.
- Two, they're private companies. They can have whatever bias and rules they want.
- Three, everybody else has a right to call them out and boycott them.
- Four, there is no role for government here. Government should stay out.

I can't believe that so many conservatives these days disagree with numbers two and four above. And I have to think that much of it relates to Trump using the First Amendment as a tool to protect his allies and punish his enemies—which in turn influences his supporters to view the First Amendment the same way. There are a couple of statistics that I think back this up. (Even though these statistics are about the news media specifically, the same kind of skepticism applies to tech companies.) First, for the last three years, the Pew Research Center has asked American adults if "criticism from news organizations keeps political leaders from doing their jobs." In 2016, only 20 percent of Republican respondents said it did. In 2017, that number jumped all the way to *56 percent*. In 2018, it was 58 percent.[39] Second, according to an August 2019 poll by *The Daily Beast*, "43 percent of self-identified Republicans said that they believed 'the president should have the authority to close news outlets engaged in bad behavior.' Only 36 percent disagreed with that statement. When asked if Trump should close down specific outlets, including CNN, *The Washington Post*, and *The New York Times*, nearly a quarter of Republicans (23 percent) agreed and 49 percent disagreed."[40]

There's no two ways about it: Because of Donald Trump, a lot of Republicans think "their guy" should be able to run roughshod over the First Amendment. I have no doubt that this has helped create a culture in which Republicans don't appreciate First Amendment rights. Take the example of a writer and professor at California State University, Fresno, Randa Jarrar, who reveled in the death of the late Barbara Bush. "Barbara Bush was a generous and smart and amazing racist who, along with her husband, raised a war criminal. Fuck outta here with your nice words," she tweeted after the former first lady's passing in 2018. "I'm happy the witch is dead. [C]an't wait for the rest of her family to fall to their demise the way 1.5 million [I]raqis have,"[41] she added in a follow-up. Those comments are so revolting. They're stomach-curdling, offensive, and incorrect—and legal. Regardless, almost 93,000 somethings—I hesitate to call all of them actual "people," because you never know on the internet—signed one of those dumb Change.org petitions calling on Cal State to fire her.[42] Should it have? The answer is absolutely not. I'm with Ben Shapiro on this one: "[H]er tweet about Barbara Bush falls squarely within the purview of free speech. It's gross. It's atrocious. But Jarrar has a right to speak, and setting the precedent that professors should be fired for saying gross, atrocious or impolitic things seems like a serious problem."[43]

This is how free speech works, my friends. It doesn't screen for the quality of a person's viewpoint. That's exactly why Alex Jones, Laura Loomer, Jacob Wohl, and the lot of 'em have the right to believe and say *whatever* messed-up, nonsensical opinions about politics they want to. It's just that Facebook and Twitter have no legal responsibility to give them their real estate to say it. Thinking otherwise is not a conservative position. It's a snowflake position.

Chapter 4

THE ENEMY OF DEMOCRACY

The Constitution is our country's defining document. It's our founding charter. It says so right there in the preamble: "We the People of the United States, in Order to form a more perfect Union, establish Justice, insure domestic Tranquility, provide for the common defense," and so on and so forth. It's also the guarantor of Americans' shared rights—to free speech, to freedom of assembly, to bear arms, to due process. But there's another way of looking at it that really gives meaning to what the United States is: The Constitution is the backbone of our democracy. It establishes a president and gives that individual certain powers and limits. It establishes a Congress and a judiciary and describes what they're there for. It tells those branches together what they can't do to private citizens. This all provides the support structure for our form of government.

If Donald Trump has demonstrated over and over again that he doesn't care about upholding this structure—that instead he'll blow holes through whatever part of it is inconvenient to him—then it's worth asking if he cares about supporting democracy at all: doing his part to make sure it works and defending it from those who attack it. The answer is such a resounding "no" that it goes a long way toward supporting my most consistent criticism of Trump: that he acts like a lawless king, unbound by the law, by the rules, by the truth, by democratic norms, by all human decency. No one who behaves like this is capable of being an advocate for or at least a caretaker of a form of government like ours.

Congress created a Department of Justice, which has the purpose to "ensure fair and impartial administration of justice for all Americans"; Trump injects political considerations into its work. Congress gave the Harry Truman administration the ability to create a Central Intelligence Agency, partly in response to the expansion of the USSR; Trump has repeatedly called into question the CIA's findings about, ironically, Russian interference in our elections. Congress created penalties for undermining the integrity of federal investigations; Trump obstructed the investigation into that aforementioned Russian interference. Entities such as the DOJ and our intelligence agencies, and criminal laws designed to make sure investigations stay on the rails, are some of the things that our Congress has created to make our particular democracy work better. Trump disregards these creations when it suits him.

If he does this on our soil, what makes anyone think he would give two you-know-whats about democracy abroad? In the past, my party has proudly stood for the freedom and dignity of people in other countries whose regimes deprive them of those God-given rights. Trump stands with the regimes, instead. He stands with Vladimir Putin of Russia, who's insulated by a network of thugs and whose political opposition and media critics often mysteriously wind up dead; he stands with Kim Jong-un of North Korea, a despot whom Trump calls his friend;[1] he stands with Xi Jinping of China, he stands with Rodrigo Duterte of the Philippines, he stands with low-life criminals who run authoritarian states that stomp on their citizens—or worse. And you know what they say about peer groups: when the character of a man is not clear, look to his friends.

All throughout his presidential term, Trump has been antagonistic, hostile, or indifferent to democracy, depending on the circumstances. This is doing long-term harm to the presidency and the United States' reputation. It's hurting us here because it's laying the groundwork for Trump imitators to inherit an office that he's made weaker and exploit it even more. It's hurting us overseas because the democratic allies we've worked with for decades to help maintain a relatively stable world and prevent the rise of another widespread, violent, totalitarian movement are looking at us like *What the hell are you doing?*

Taken together, this provides a case that Trump not only is unfit to be president but should be disqualified from continuing to do the job. His bizarre obsessions, character defects, and constant lapses in judgment about even the most basic government functions—which directly limit his ability to do his duty—make him unsuited to be the chief executive at a personal level. But the *things he's done* that run afoul of democracy make it clear that he can't be trusted with all the buttons and levers that make it go.

OBSTRUCTING JUSTICE

One of the most flagrant examples of this is Trump's obstruction of the investigation into Russia's meddling with the 2016 presidential election. Let me bracket this by saying that I know that everything about Special Counsel Robert Mueller is so partisan that it's become really, really difficult for people of any political stripe to look at his work and the results of that work *for what they are*. Not for what partisan takeaways we get about what the Democrats got wrong or the Republicans got right, or vice versa; not for what the media overplayed or underplayed; not for what they confirmed or disproved about our expectations; but for what *actually* happened. Mueller is an officer of the law, he collected sworn testimony and facts, and he used it to write a big ol' four-hundred-page-plus report. That's it. Let's look at what that report tells us.

What it tells us is that Russia did indeed interfere in our election to try to benefit Trump's chances of winning; Trump's campaign was aware of and welcomed the help; and the Trump *administration*, led by Trump himself, obstructed Mueller's inquiry into that breach of our election security and integrity in several ways. That is the record. Period. Trump has claimed that the probe was nothing more than a "witch hunt," but remember the question I asked about him or his lackeys ever backing up their charges of "fake news" with evidence? Trump and his lackeys have not provided evidence that Mueller's findings of obstruction didn't happen. They only *say* that. I choose to believe hard evidence over empty rhetoric. (I always thought conservatives prided themselves on doing the same thing.)

Here's what that hard evidence states, straight from the Mueller report to your eyes:

In mid-January 2017, incoming National Security Advisor Michael Flynn falsely denied to the Vice President, other administration officials, and FBI agents that he had talked to Russian Ambassador Sergey Kislyak about

Russia's response to U.S. sanctions on Russia for its election interference. . . . Later that afternoon [February 14], the President cleared the Oval Office to have a one-on-one meeting with [former FBI director James] Comey. Referring to the FBI's investigation of Flynn, the President said, "I hope you can see your way clear to letting this go, to letting Flynn go. He is a good guy. I hope you can let this go." . . . After Comey's account of the President's request to "let Flynn go" became public, the President publicly disputed several aspects of the story. . . . Despite those denials, substantial evidence corroborates Comey's account.[2]

On Saturday, June 17, 2017, the President called [former White House counsel Don] McGahn and directed him to have the Special Counsel removed. McGahn was at home and the President was at Camp David. In interviews with this Office, McGahn recalled that the President called him at home twice and on both occasions directed him to call [former deputy attorney general Rod] Rosenstein and say that Mueller had conflicts that precluded him from serving as Special Counsel. . . . When the President called McGahn a second time to follow up on the order to call the Department of Justice, McGahn recalled that the President was more direct, saying something like, "Call Rod, tell Rod that Mueller has conflicts and can't be the Special Counsel." McGahn recalled the President telling him "Mueller has to go" and "Call me back when you do it." . . . McGahn is a credible witness with no motive to lie or exaggerate given the position he held in the White House.[3]

On January 26, 2018, the President's personal counsel called McGahn's attorney and said that the President wanted McGahn to put out a statement denying that he had been asked to fire the Special Counsel and that he had threatened to quit in protest. McGahn's attorney spoke with McGahn about that request and then called the President's personal counsel to relay that McGahn would not make a statement. McGahn's attorney informed the President's personal counsel that the Times story was accurate in reporting that the President wanted the Special Counsel removed. . . .

Also on January 26, 201[8], [former White House communications director Hope] Hicks recalled that the President asked [former White House press secretary Sarah Huckabee] Sanders to contact McGahn about the story. McGahn told Sanders there was no need to respond and indicated that some of the article was accurate. . . .

[O]n February 5, 2018, the President complained about the *Times* article to [former White House staff secretary Rob] Porter. The President told Porter that the article was "bullshit" and he had not sought to terminate the Special Counsel. The President said that McGahn leaked to the media to make himself look good. The President then directed Porter to tell McGahn to create a record to make clear that the President never directed McGahn to fire the Special Counsel. Porter thought the matter should be handled by the White House communications office, but the President said he wanted McGahn to write a letter to the file "for our records" and wanted something beyond a press statement to demonstrate that the reporting was inaccurate. The President referred to McGahn as a "lying bastard" and said that he wanted a record from him. Porter recalled the President saying something to the effect of, "If he doesn't write a letter, then maybe I'll have to get rid of him."

Later that day, Porter spoke to McGahn to deliver the President's message. Porter told McGahn that he had to write a letter to dispute that he was ever ordered to terminate the Special Counsel. McGahn shrugged off the request, explaining that the media reports were true. . . . Porter told McGahn that the President suggested that McGahn would be fired if he did not write the letter. . . .

The next day, on February 6, 2018, [former White House chief of staff John] Kelly scheduled time for McGahn to meet with him and the President in the Oval Office to discuss the Times article. . . .

The President began the Oval Office meeting by telling McGahn that the New York Times story did not "look good" and McGahn needed to correct it. McGahn recalled the President said, "I never said to fire Mueller. I never said 'fire.'" . . .

As previously described . . . substantial evidence supports McGahn's account that the President had directed him to have the Special Counsel removed, including the timing and context of the President's directive; the manner in which McGahn reacted; and the fact that the President had been told the conflicts were insubstantial, were being considered by the Department of Justice, and should be raised with the President's personal counsel rather than brought to McGahn. In addition, the President's subsequent denials that he had told McGahn to have the Special Counsel removed were carefully worded. When first asked about the New York Times story, the President said, 'Fake news, folks. Fake news. A typical New York Times fake story.' And when the President spoke with McGahn in the Oval Office, he focused on whether he had used the word "fire," saying, "I never said to fire Mueller. I never said 'fire'" and "Did I say the word 'fire'?" The President's assertion in the Oval Office meeting that he had never directed McGahn to have the Special Counsel removed thus runs counter to the evidence.[4]

These are three blatant, clear-cut cases of Trump obstructing justice.[5] I brought up another one of them in a previous chapter, about Trump trying to influence Paul Manafort's cooperation with the investigation. You look at this conduct, and it is not aboveboard, folks. It is—bottom line—interference with a federal law enforcement investigation. I want to quote Paul Rosenzweig, a lecturer in law at George Washington University and deputy assistant secretary for policy at the Department of Homeland Security under George W. Bush: "Obstruction of justice and perjury are far more important than most normal crimes. They go to the absolute core of how the rule of law functions in this society. . . . The system itself is designed to find the truth. Obstruction of justice undercuts the very foundations of the trial system, of the jury system, by denying the people who are going to decide what happened access to the truth."[6]

Presidents do not undercut the law like this. Conservatives don't do it. As Rosenzweig added, "The rule of law that I understand to be the core of a conservative American principle, is one that requires consistency across time. It means that you apply the same rules to everybody."[7]

You know who does do nonsense like this? Crime bosses. Tyrants. People who think they're above the law do this.

LOVING HIM SOME DICTATORS

Hey, speaking of! Here are two columns, one of them listing the foreign leaders and organizations that Trump has treated with scorn, the other listing the foreign leaders and organizations that he's tried to befriend or express admiration for:

TRUMP'S SHIT LIST	TRUMP'S CRUSHES
The United Kingdom and former prime minister and Conservative Party leader Theresa May [8]	Kim Jong-un, dictator of North Korea
Germany and German chancellor Angela Merkel, arguably the most powerful democratic leader outside the United States	Xi Jinping, leader of Communist China
Canada, the United States' second-largest trading partner [9]	Rodrigo Duterte, president of the Philippines, who supports the extrajudicial murder of even petty criminals [11]
Mexico, the United States' third-largest trading partner [10]	Vladimir Putin, who sucks
Pretty much all of Latin America	Recep Tayyip Erdoğan, president of Turkey, who suppresses dissent and aggressively censors speech [12]
NATO, the world's most powerful military alliance	

Do you notice anything funny about those two columns? Anything strike you as odd?

Look, I can kid a little about this, but there isn't anything in those two columns that has been exaggerated for comedic effect. It's just reality. Trump has tested the United States' *most significant partnerships* internationally. He has bashed NATO—which helps keep Putin in check and adds meaning to our relationship with Europe, the world's biggest cluster of democracies—since he was first a candidate for the Republican presidential nomination. Susan Glasser of *The New Yorker* interviewed ten senior German officials for a story about Trump's relationship with Merkel and reported this:

> The President, the German officials concluded, harbored a deep animus toward Germany in general, and Merkel in particular. "There's a single-mindedness to it and almost an obsession, it seems, and this is something we are hearing from colleagues in the Administration, too: an obsession with Germany," one of the senior German officials told me. "It seems like it's very often issues that can seemingly be boiled down to a single number, like two per cent [spending on NATO], or to a single concept. . . . He latches on to that with a certain fixation." Niels Annen, a Bundestag member who is the German equivalent of the Deputy Secretary of State, told me, "Unfortunately, Germany seems to be very high on the agenda of the President himself."[13]

You can make the argument that Germany and other European countries should foot more of the bill for NATO—but you can't think about getting out of NATO altogether.[14] You can criticize Merkel and not agree with the way she's handled Europe's refugee crisis in her own nation—but you can't let your opinion of her torpedo a crucial strategic relationship. You can't be the president of the United States and treat your closest democratic allies across the Atlantic as though they are an annoyance and have them end up looking at you as though you're a complete dumbass.

Trump neither understands nor appreciates this. Instead, he prefers the rogues like himself who go it alone, break the rules, and *really* retaliate against their political adversaries. People such as Chairman Kim, who runs a family murder business. Freedom House, a pro-democracy human rights group, describes his regime like this: "North Korea is a one-party state led by a dynastic totalitarian dictatorship. Surveillance is pervasive, arbitrary arrests and detention are common, and punishments for political offenses are severe. The state maintains a system of camps for political prisoners where torture, forced labor, starvation, and other atrocities take place."[15] A UN Human Rights Council report from 2014 found "systematic, widespread and gross human rights violations" in the country, "many" of which "entailed crimes against humanity based on State policies." The Kim regime "has used food as a means of control over the population," "imposes on citizens where they must live and work," orchestrates "almost complete denial of the right to freedom of thought, conscience and religion, as well as of the rights to freedom of opinion, expression, information and association," and "disappears" political foes to prison camps without due process.

"In the political prison camps of the Democratic People's Republic of Korea," the UN report elaborated, "the inmate population has been gradually eliminated through deliberate starvation, forced labour, executions, torture, rape and the denial of reproductive rights enforced through punishment, forced abortion and infanticide. The commission estimates that hundreds of thousands of political prisoners have perished in these camps over the past five decades. The unspeakable atrocities that are being committed against inmates of the *kwanliso* political prison camps resemble the horrors of camps that totalitarian States established during the twentieth century."[16]

Trump explained Kim's barbarity by telling Fox News anchor Bret Baier, "Well he's a tough guy."

He complimented Kim for inheriting the regime from his dad, Kim Jong-il: "You take it over from your father—I don't care who you are, what you are, how much of an advantage you have. If you can do that at 27 years old, that's one in 10,000 that could do that."[17]

Trump absolved Kim of blame for the death of American student Otto Warmbier, who died shortly after experiencing seventeen months in North Korean captivity: "Some really bad things happened to Otto—some really, really bad things. But Kim tells me that he didn't know about it, and I will take him at his word."[18]

Trump said he "smiled when [Kim] called Swampman Joe Biden a low IQ individual."[19]

He's joked about being pen pals with Kim: "He wrote me beautiful letters and they're great letters. We fell in love."[20]

He said that "Chariman [*sic*] Kim has a great and beautiful vision for his country," and that "He will do the right thing because he is far too smart not to, and he does not want to disappoint his friend, President Trump!"[21]

"His friend."

The Art of the Deal can go fuck itself if it means befriending a despot. And I really think it's appropriate to tell Trump to do the same.

Let's see, who else ... there's General Secretary Xi, of China.

In October 2019, Trump tweeted, "Congratulations to

President Xi and the Chinese people on the 70th Anniversary of the People's Republic of China!"[22]

The People's Republic of China is a Communist dictatorship, created by Mao Zedong, that is responsible for the deaths of millions. Its current "president for life," Xi, operates a cult of personality. "Thousands of Christians in an impoverished county in rural southeast China have swapped their posters of Jesus for portraits of President Xi Jinping as part of a local government poverty-relief programme that seeks to 'transform believers in religion into believers in the party,'" the *South China Morning Post*, Hong Kong's leading newspaper, reported in 2017.[23]

His crackdown on religious expression is comprehensive: an American-based Christian nonprofit and a Chinese pastor documented the Chinese government "destroying crosses, burning bibles, shutting churches and ordering followers to sign papers renouncing their faith" in 2018, according to the Associated Press, and it has built reeducation camps and a surveillance system to monitor millions of Muslim-minority people. The imprisonment rates in such regions have swelled, the *New York Times* reported in 2019.[24] A 2018 report from our own Congress—the bipartisan Congressional-Executive Commission on China—documented a "dire human rights situation inside China and the continued downward trajectory, by virtually every measure, since Xi Jinping became Communist Party General Secretary in 2012 and President in 2013."[25] Xi made himself president for life in 2018.[26]

Trump said that Xi "is a great leader who very much has the respect of his people. He is also a good man in a 'tough business.'"[27]

As for the others:

- The antidrug policy of President Rodrigo Duterte of the Philippines features untold numbers of extrajudicial killings—either by police or by private individuals acting with some kind of government sanction. The government's official count of all drug war–related deaths since 2016 is 6,600; human rights groups peg the statistic at more than three times as high.[28] According to an official White House transcript, the first thing Trump said after exchanging pleasantries with Duterte during a phone call in 2017 was "I just wanted to congratulate you because I am hearing of the unbelievable job on the drug problem. Many countries have the problem, we have a problem, but what a great job you are doing and I just wanted to call and tell you that."[29]

- It's widely accepted that President Recep Tayyip Erdoğan of Turkey is responsible for democracy in retreat in his country. "After initially passing some liberalizing reforms, [his] government showed growing contempt for political rights and civil liberties, and its authoritarian nature has been fully consolidated since a 2016 coup attempt triggered a more dramatic crackdown on perceived opponents of the leadership. Constitutional changes adopted in 2017 concentrated power in the hands of the president, and worsening electoral conditions have made it increasingly difficult for opposition parties to challenge Erdoğan's control," Freedom House reported in 2019.[30] Amid that development, Trump complimented Erdoğan on "running a very difficult part of the world" and "getting very high marks" for it.[31] In 2019, Trump called Erdoğan a "friend of mine, somebody I've become very close to, in many respects, and he's doing a very good job."[32]

- And as for Vladimir Putin, well . . .

Putin probably deserves more than just a bullet point. In fact, it was Trump's wimpy, traitorous behavior around him in Helsinki in July 2018 that caused me to dump Trump for good. Forgive me for quoting myself, but the way I put it exactly was: "Trump asked just now who he believes, his own intelligence agencies or Putin. He won't answer. But he speaks more favorably of Putin. TRUMP WON'T STAND WITH HIS OWN COUNTRY. That's it. That should be the final straw. It is for me."[33]

I think it's worth citing in full the Q and A with a journalist that led me to state that. It was during a joint press conference— Putin was right by his side. Trump is six foot three. Putin is five foot seven. But you tell me which man seemed to stand taller.

Question: President Trump, you first. Just now, President Putin denied having anything to do with the election interference in 2016. Every U.S. intelligence agency has concluded that Russia did. What—who—my first question for you, sir, is, who do you believe?

My second question is, would you now, with the whole world watching, tell President Putin—would you denounce what happened in 2016? And would you warn him to never do it again?

President Trump: So let me just say that we have two thoughts. You have groups that are wondering why the FBI never took the server. Why haven't they taken the server? Why was the FBI told to leave the office of the Democratic National Committee? I've been wondering that. I've been asking that for months and months, and I've been tweeting it out and calling it out on social media. Where is the server? I want to know, where is the server? And what is the server saying?

With that being said, all I can do is ask the question.

My people came to me—Dan Coats came to me and some others—they said they think it's Russia. I have President Putin; he just said it's not Russia.

I will say this: I don't see any reason why it would be, but I really do want to see the server. But I have—I have confidence in both parties. I really believe that this will probably go on for a while, but I don't think it can go on without finding out what happened to the server. . . .

So I have great confidence in my intelligence people, but I will tell you that President Putin was extremely strong and powerful in his denial today.[34]

On the world stage, Donald Trump favored the Russian thug whose people interfered in our election process over the intelligence people in his own government who concluded, definitively, that the Russian thug was guilty. I don't care if Trump weakly tried to clear up his long-winded comment a day later, saying he had meant to say "wouldn't" when he had said "I don't see any reason why it would be."[35] He can't clarify his way out of being a mealy-mouthed coward.

Donald. Trump. Does. Not. Promote. American. Interests. Period.

CANCELING ELECTIONS

I'll mention this part briefly; it's pretty timely to mention strongmen and dictators like this during election season here at home. Again, Xi recently made himself president for life; Erdoğan turned his democracy, with checks and balances, into a one-man show, starring him; and Putin will have been Russian president for twenty years, with a four-year break, by the time his term ends in 2024. These are men who found ways to consolidate their power by rigging the political system against their challengers. So would it surprise you to learn that the Trumpified Republican Party has been proactive in trying to eliminate diversity of viewpoint in its ranks and quash dissent?

- In January 2019, the Republican National Committee adopted a resolution offering "its undivided support for President Donald J. Trump and his effective Presidency,"[36] which isn't the norm before actually nominating the guy. (It wasn't that long ago that Lyndon B. Johnson, a sitting Democratic president, bowed out during his reelection campaign in a primary fight that he looked destined to lose.) The resolution also called Trump a "courageous leader for the American People," which, after reading all that dictator love a few pages ago, is a complete joke, but whatever.

- In February, the Associated Press reported that the Trump campaign was "taking steps to change state party rules, crowd out potential rivals and quell any early signs of opposition that could embarrass the president." The story added that it "has used endorsements, lobbying and rule changes to increase the likelihood that only loyal Trump activists make it to the Republican nominating convention in August 2020," and it "plans to organize at county and state caucuses and conventions over the next 18 months to elevate pro-Trump leaders and potential delegates . . . [and] aims to have complete control of the convention agenda, rules and platform—and to identify any potential troublemakers well in advance."[37]

▌ In the summer of 2019, various states started canceling
their primary elections and caucuses. South Carolina—a
key early primary state every four years—Nevada, and
Kansas were the first.[38] Arizona followed.[39] Then
Alaska.[40] Then Minnesota's state GOP decided that
Trump would be the only Republican candidate listed on
the presidential primary ballot in March 2020. So did the
state GOPs in Georgia and North Carolina.[41]

These are not the signs of a confident president; they're the
signs of a weak one, who wants to make it easier to hold on to
his power. That's the exact type of attitude that pissed Republicans off in 2010 during the Tea Party wave and in 2016 on
the way to Trump's election—it was all about throwing out the
bums who were desperate to cling to their offices. Who knows?
Maybe the swamp has gotten the better of Trump?

Chapter 5

THE CULTIST

et's do a quick compare-and-contrast involving some world history. I'm going to excerpt a few passages from an ode to Josef Stalin written by a contemporary Soviet author named A. O. Avidenko.[1] Below each excerpt, I'm going to place a quotation from someone in Trump World in praise of Trump—a "mini-ode," if you will. When you read the quotes in each pair, think about how similar they are on a scale of 1 to 10. (I'll get into what that scale measures in a minute.) Here we go:

• • •

"I shall be eternally happy and joyous, all thanks to thee, great educator, Stalin. Everything belongs to thee, chief of our great country."

"Have a great weekend. The president makes such a thing possible for us all."
—Fox Business host Lou Dobbs, September 13, 2019[2]

•••

"The men of all ages will call on thy name, which is strong, beautiful, wise and marvelous."

> *"President Trump has a magnetic personality and exudes positive energy, which is infectious to those around him. He has an unparalleled ability to communicate with people, whether he is speaking to a room of three or an arena of 30,000. He has built great relationships throughout his life and treats everyone with respect. He is brilliant with a great sense of humor . . . and an amazing ability to make people feel special and aspire to be more than even they thought possible."*
>
> —former White House director of strategic communications
> Hope Hicks, May 30, 2017[3]

•••

"Every time I have found myself in [Stalin's] presence I have been subjugated by his strength, his charm, his grandeur. I have experienced a great desire to sing, to cry out, to shout with joy and happiness."

> *"The President was treated like a Rock Star inside the hospital, which was all caught on video. They all loved seeing their great President!"*
>
> —White House social media director Dan Scavino,
> August 7, 2019, after Trump's visit to a Dayton, Ohio,
> hospital that had received mass shooting victims[4]

These tributes are all too damn close for comfort to one another. You have a major cable news personality and Trump lackey saying that Trump himself is due credit for making Americans' downtime "great," which is creepy as hell and a depressing way to see life; the president's spokeswoman calling Trump all but the greatest thing since sliced bread; and Trump's chief Twitter henchman saying that families in a hospital ward treated Trump like a "Rock Star" and "loved seeing their great President"—while they grieved loved ones who had just been slain in an incident of mass slaughter. On a scale of 1 to 10—on which 1 was normal political speech in a free society and 10 was pure propaganda—A. O. Avidenko scored a perfect 10.

Lou Dobbs, Hope Hicks, and Dan Scavino combined to get about 100 percent of the way to a perfect 10 themselves.

Their rhetoric is the rhetoric of cults. Period. Cults in which the central figure is someone who can do no wrong—like Trump, whose campaign secretary, Kayleigh McEnany, said he has never lied to Americans[5]—and has total authority—like Trump, whose Republican Party chairwoman, Ronna McDaniel, dismissed Republican challengers to him by saying, "So have at it, go ahead, waste your money, waste your time and go ahead and lose."[6] That's the thing about this over-the-top adulation of Trump: It's not just Dobbs, Hicks, Scavino, McEnany, and McDaniel, it's Sean Hannity, *Fox & Friends*, Mark Levin, the official news channel of alternate reality One America News Network, and his other news allies; it's Jerry Falwell, Jr., Robert Jeffress, Franklin Graham, televangelist James Robison, and the other Christian leaders who go all in for him; it's the politicians who have sold out their conservative virtues completely, including the House Freedom Caucus, Lindsey Graham, Newt Gingrich, and a rotating cast of D-list Republicans (such as Matt Gaetz) and bizarre social media celebrities for whom facts are utterly optional ("Diamond and Silk," Charlie Kirk, Jacob Wohl). The examples from this cast of characters are so numerous that they could fill a book all by themselves. And they go from being nausea inducing to being a genuinely alarming threat to the country; they abet the creation of a leader who presents himself as flawless and give him the cover he craves to do whatever he wants. They make him into someone who walks around as though there's a halo over his head.

But Joe, weren't there pictures of Obama in which it looked as though he actually *had a halo over his head?* I know which ones you're talking about: the ones from the Associated Press, in which the presidential seal is behind Obama's head and that the AP explained as having an unintentional "halo effect" that had been a problem photographing George W. Bush during his presidency, too.[7] Then there was the issue of *Newsweek* that declared Obama the "first gay president" and whose cover depicted Obama with a rainbow-colored halo directly over his head.[8] It wasn't just images, either: a *Politico* story from the 2008 campaign headlined "Messianic Rhetoric Infuses Obama Rallies" included the statement "Obama's wife, Michelle, opened the rally with a description of her husband that could, at moments, have been a description of Jesus Christ."[9] *Newsweek* later referred to Obama's second term as "The Second Coming." The iconography around Obama was uncomfortable—and an indication, I think, that our presidential politics were getting more cultish even before Trump hopped onto the stage.

Cult of personality is wrong. The worshipping of any politician—Obama or Trump—is dangerous. But the difference from then to now is that Trump has an army of high-profile, fibbing, shameless toadies around him—people who are not just spinning for him but outright spreading disinformation and falsehoods on his behalf and going to the mat for him in the most contorted of ways.

I mean, *good lord*, just look at the tale of the tape, starting at the top: Trump's first meeting with his full cabinet, in June 2017, included his calling individually on his subordinates, several of whom, in turn, lathered him with praise.

You had Vice President Mike Pence, an absolute lapdog, looking Trump in the eye across a table and saying "just the greatest privilege of my life is to serve as vice president to a president who's keeping his word to the American people."[10]

You had Reince Priebus, then Trump's chief of staff, saying "On behalf of the entire senior staff around you, Mr. President, we thank you for the opportunity and the blessing that you've given us to serve your agenda and the American people."[11]

You had Tom Price, his short-lived secretary of health and human services, saying "What an incredible honor it is to lead the Department of Health and Human Services at this pivotal time under your leadership. I can't thank you enough for the privilege that you've given me."[12]

This kind of slobbering is some real bend-down-and-kiss-the-ring bullshit. And the types of leaders who do it are more kinglike than they are garden-variety elected representatives. Dartmouth College government professor Brendan Nyhan told NPR at the time of the cabinet lovefest that the display was "a more common occurrence in nondemocratic regimes which are trying to portray themselves as being popular." Without the benefit of foresight, he said also that he didn't "want to make too much of one Cabinet meeting."[13] That's understandable. But the sycophancy hasn't stopped since that "one cabinet meeting"—instead it's been repeated many times over and become all the more ridiculous with age.

Just compare Pence's soft-spoken adulation in that June 2017 gathering, which was bad enough, to his over-the-top flattery of the president six months later in another get-together of the president's deputies. *Washington Post* reporter Aaron Blake crunched the numbers: "By the end, Pence offered 14 separate commendations for Trump in less than three minutes—math that works out to one every 12.5 seconds. And each bit of praise was addressed directly to Trump, who was seated directly across the table."[14] I'd repeat all fourteen here, but I'd puke. Let's take just three of them: "I'm deeply humbled, as your vice president, to be able to be here." "You've spurred an optimism in this country that's setting records." "Mostly, Mr. President, I'll end where I began and just tell you, I want to thank you, Mr. President. I want to thank you for speaking on behalf of and fighting every day for the forgotten men and women of America."

Just read that again: "I'll end where I began," which really means "Restating, for the record, that I couldn't be more grateful to slurp your boots."

That kind of slavish behavior from Trump's inner circle—giving thanks as if Trump is the source of divine rights—is only one way the cult communicates. Another is how it showers the president with superlatives—not just compliments but words that make it seem as though Trump has the very best of some human ability or quality. Here again: that's Stalinist.

"In the Soviet press you may find [Stalin] fulsomely called 'Great,' 'Beloved,' 'Bold,' 'Wise,' 'Inspirer,' 'Genius.' . . . In speeches he has been addressed by ordinarily uneffusive folk as, 'Our Best Collective Farmer Worker,' 'Our Shockworker, Our Best of Best,' and 'Our Darling, Our Guiding Star.' Celebrations have concluded with the words, 'Long Live Our Dear Leader, Our Warmly Beloved Stalin, Our Comrade, Our Friend,'" wrote the historian John Gunther in *Inside Europe*.[15]

Stephen Miller, a senior adviser to Trump, went with "political genius" and so much more during an infamous interview with CNN journalist Jake Tapper in January 2018. "You know, on the campaign, I had the chance to travel all across the country with the president on Trump Force One. It would be the president, me, Dan Scavino, Hope Hicks, a few other people going from rally to rally to rally to rally. And I saw a man who was a political genius, somebody who we would be going down, landing in descent, there would be a breaking news development. And in 20 minutes, he would dictate 10 paragraphs of new material to address that event, and then deliver flawlessly in front of an audience of 10,000 people."

He continued, "The reality is, is the president is a political genius who won against a field of 17 incredibly talented people, who took down the Bush dynasty, who took down the Clinton dynasty, who took down the entire media complex with its 90 percent negative coverage, took down billions of dollars in special interests donations. And he did it all through the people and through his strategy and his vision and his insight and his experience."[16]

For Stephen Miller, there clearly aren't enough positive adjectives to describe an authoritarian at the center of a cult of personality. And yes, that's how I would describe the undemocratic, unpatriotic mess that Donald Trump has gotten us into, with his unquenchable demand for love and loyalty, no matter the circumstances. And I really mean "no matter the circumstances." The episode I referred to a few paragraphs back involving Scavino, the Trump social media guru, and the Dayton shooting in August 2019 that took the lives of ten people and injured twenty-seven others provides the most extreme kind of evidence. Trump visited first responders and some of the victims at Miami Valley Regional Hospital a few days after the tragedy, alongside Ohio senator Sherrod Brown and Dayton mayor Nan Whaley, both Democrats, among other Ohio officials. Reporters were barred from accompanying the president.[17]

Though both Brown and Whaley said they had urged Trump to lead on gun control efforts in Washington and criticized his rhetorical habits, they complimented his behavior during the visit. "He was received well by the patients, as you would expect. They're hurting," Brown said. "He was comforting, he did the right things, and Melania did the right things. It's his job, in part, to comfort people. I'm glad he did it in those hospital rooms."[18] Whaley added that Trump "was very nice" and was "treated well by the victims"[19] and that it was a "good decision" for him not to stop by the city district where the shooting occurred. "I think a lot of people that own businesses in that district aren't interested in the president being there. And a lot of the time his talk can be very divisive, and that's the last thing we need in Dayton."

On the whole, Brown and Whaley described Trump's visit to the hospital as positive and *well received*.

Keep that in mind, because this is how Scavino responded on Twitter:

Very SAD to see Ohio Senator Brown, & Dayton Mayor Nan Whaley - LYING & completely mischaracterizing what took place w/ the President's visit to Miami Valley Hospital today. They are disgraceful politicians, doing nothing but politicizing a mass shooting, at every turn they can. . . . The President was treated like a Rock Star inside the hospital, which was all caught on video. They all loved seeing their great President![20]

White House Press Secretary Stephanie Grisham then piggybacked on Scavino's comment, quoting him on Twitter and tweeting this:

President @realDonaldTrump graciously asked Sen Brown & Mayor Whaley to join as he and the First Lady visited victims, medical staff & first responders. It is genuinely sad to see them immediately hold such a dishonest press conference in the name of partisan politics.[21]

Again: Brown and Whaley were "dishonest" about what? What did they mischaracterize? In what way did they say Trump was greeted with anything but—
Wait, then Trump tweeted about it?

Just left Dayton, Ohio, where I met with the Victims & families, Law Enforcement, Medical Staff & First Responders. It was a warm & wonderful visit. Tremendous enthusiasm & even Love. Then I saw failed Presidential Candidate (0%) Sherrod Brown & Mayor Whaley totally . . . misrepresenting what took place inside of the hospital. Their news conference after I left for El Paso was a fraud. It bore no resemblance to what took place with those incredible people that I was so lucky to meet and spend time with. They were all amazing![22]

The news conference was a "fraud"? It "bore no resemblance" to reality? How?
If you can bear with this for just a paragraph longer . . . Trump elaborated on his tweets a while later after he landed in El Paso to visit first responders who had attended to the victims

of the mass shooting there, which preceded the one in Dayton by a day.

> [Brown and Whaley] shouldn't be politicking today. They couldn't believe what they saw, and they said it to people. They've never seen anything like it. The entire hospital, no different than what we had in El Paso, the entire hospital, I mean, everybody was so proud of the job they did. . . . We made the tour, they couldn't believe it—she said it to people, he said it to people. I get on Air Force One—where they do have a lot of televisions—I turn on the television, and there they are, saying, "Well, I don't know if it was appropriate for the president to be here, you know," etc., etc., the same old line.[23]

Brown and Whaley did not say that.

"And they're very dishonest people," Trump continued, "and that's probably why [Brown] got, I think, about 0 percent, then he failed as a presidential candidate."

Think about where this started, where it went, and where it ended: It started with Brown and Whaley saying Trump had been "received well" and "treated well" by the shooting victims; it continued with Scavino saying that Brown and Whaley were "lying and completely mischaracterizing" Trump's visit; it then went to Grisham saying they had held a "dishonest press conference"; it progressed further to Trump saying he had seen with his own two eyes Brown and Whaley "totally misrepresenting what took place inside of the hospital"; and it concluded with Trump reaffirming that he had seen something that hadn't happened in reality, and by the way, did you know Brown is a political failure, big league?

Think back to Trump's falsified Hurricane Dorian charts one more time: Trump either willfully misrepresents or doesn't realize he misrepresents what's happening in the real world. In each case, he propped up his own ego. Also in each case, he had deputies prop it up for good measure—the national security aide on Dorian, Scavino and Grisham here. Let's put this together, people: Trump leads an apparatus that helps him lie to boost his image. If that isn't a cult . . .

Again, we come across the questions: Why does any of this matter? Why are his personality defects, even those as glaring and disturbing as this one, more significant than putting conservative judges on the court or fulfilling some other right-of-center political goal?

First, I don't understand why anyone would think it's okay that the president of the United States is a committed liar, completely delusional, or maybe both. We've given away the game if we think it's all right to trade Republican policy victories for a cult of personality that resembles the totalitarian regimes the United States has almost always opposed. That's a matter of principle, sure. But it's also a warning. Take it from Brian Klaas, a widely cited democracy expert who teaches at the London School of Economics:

> First, in order to roll back democratic checks, despots must blur the lines between truth and falsehood. This makes it difficult to ascertain who to trust in times of crisis. Throughout history, *this graying of truth often starts on trivial matters, particularly on issues that surround the cult of personality associated with the leader.* . . . Like many despots, Trump is unable to accept popular narratives that challenges [*sic*] his standing as the man of the people.

This blurring of the truth becomes dangerous when real crises break out. If China makes a claim about the South China Sea and Trump makes the opposite claim, how can Americans—or American allies—trust the White House? After all, if Trump's team lies about an easily disproved claim where citizens can simply look at side-by-side photos, what about statements that aren't easily verifiable with photographs?

And yet, in spite of these risks, despots thrive on this uncertainty. Blurring that line between fact and falsehood dilutes critiques and ensures that citizens question the nature of truth itself. (My emphasis.)[24]

Most Americans have a dim view of Trump's temperament and trustworthiness. Seventy percent of American adults surveyed in September 2018 said they would not describe him as "even-tempered," reported the Pew Research Center.[25] Sixty-five percent of American adults surveyed in June 2019 said they would not describe him as honest or trustworthy, reported Gallup.[26] What happens when Trump goes off the rails about a national security crisis? A real threat of war? Do we trust an ill-tempered liar to make the right decision—and do we trust him to tell the truth about the effectiveness of that decision or admit if the decision is wrong, when he leads a cult that insists to the public he is only ever right?

Cults also get people to surrender their values and core principles, which should matter quite a bit to conservatives. Ruth Ben-Ghiat, a professor at New York University who is a world-leading expert on authoritarianism, has this to say: "[L]ike Putin and [Italy's Silvio] Berlusconi, Trump's appeal is less intellectual than emotional. No matter if few of his political ideas are original. It's the way he presents those ideas—as an extension of his own personality and passion, rather than any party platform—that wins people over."[27]

What a surprise, then, that when Trump told four brown-skinned US congresswomen to "go back to where they came from," Republicans said nothing—and when he announced a budget deal in July 2019 that added trillions of dollars to the national debt and busted all spending caps, Republicans said nothing, either. What a surprise that the number of Republican adults who say the country's problems could be solved more effectively if presidents didn't have to worry so much about Congress or the courts increased from 14 percent in 2016 to 43 percent in 2019, according to Pew.[28] What a surprise that cult grifters such as Charlie Kirk of Turning Point USA tweeted in 2016, "Free markets, free people," and then tweeted in 2019 support for Trump signing "an executive order banning tech companies from getting federal contracts due to viewpoint discrimination."[29] What a surprise that Rush Limbaugh went pro-tariff—even though tariffs are tax increases, hurt the American people, and generally are shitty policy.[30]

And what a surprise that Thom Tillis, a Republican senator from North Carolina, published an op-ed on February 25, 2019, that opposed Trump's emergency declaration on the southern border[31]—the conservative, checks-and-balances thing to do—and then three weeks later changed his mind, obviously a result of the Trump cult threatening to come for his seat. "We're not happy with the way Senator Tillis seems not to support the president," said one North Carolina GOP county chairwoman. Notice how she said support "the president," not "conservative principles."[32]

It's. A. Cult.

When you buy into the cult, you'll say just about anything to back it. You'll believe just about anything to support it. But heaven help us when people start *doing* just about anything to keep it going. I want to close this chapter with a reminder about the whistle-blower who told the chairmen of the House and Senate Intelligence Committees that he had an "urgent concern" about "information from multiple U.S. Government officials that the President of the United States is using the power of his office to solicit interference from a foreign country in the 2020 U.S. election." Included in the whistle-blower's complaint was his belief that Trump "sought to pressure the Ukrainian leader [Volodymyr Zelensky] to take actions to help the President's 2020 reelection bid"[33] during a phone call in July 2019—which was borne out by a transcript of the call that the White House released itself. The background is complicated, so I'll let ABC News, which interviewed the relevant people on the record—meaning this comes from publicly available knowledge—take over for a minute:

> During the call, a rough summary of which was released by the White House Wednesday, Trump repeatedly encouraged Zelenskiy to work with Attorney General William Barr and his personal attorney, Rudy Giuliani, to probe [former Vice President Joe] Biden's role in the dismissal of the country's prosecutor general, Viktor Shokin, in 2016.
>
> In an interview with ABC News in April 2019, Shokin said he believed Biden pressured the government to fire him because he was leading an investigation into Burisma, a Ukrainian oil and gas company where Biden's son, Hunter, had a seat on the board of directors.
>
> But the assertion that Biden acted to help his son

has been undercut by widespread criticism of Shokin from several high-profile international leaders, including members of the European Union and International Monetary Fund, who said Biden's recommendation was well justified and that Shokin had been removed because of widely shared concerns he was obstructing efforts to root out entrenched corruption in his office and Ukraine's judicial system.[34]

Not until 2019 was there ever an issue about Shokin's firing. And the fact that it became one did not arise from any new information. It was just Trump asking the Ukrainian president to have his government investigate the family of Trump's political rival on the cusp of the Democratic primary season. "There's a lot of talk about Biden's son, that Biden stopped the prosecution and a lot of people want to find out about that so whatever you can do with the Attorney General [William Barr] would be great," Trump told Zelensky during the call. "Biden went around bragging that he stopped the prosecution so if you can look into it. . . . It sounds horrible to me."[35]

The whistle-blower claimed further that "senior White House officials had intervened to 'lock down' all records of the phone call,"[36] and Trump aides, both official and unofficial—including his personal lawyer, Rudy Giuliani—met Ukrainian government officials to discuss the call further. It's not as though the call was the end of the matter—or the beginning of it, for that matter.

All of this is to say that the whistle-blower reported a troubling pattern relevant to our national security through the proper channels, and the big kahuna of that pattern was proved publicly shortly thereafter—something for which I thought at the time Trump should be impeached.[37] But the way Trump responded cinched the case for impeachment further, if such a thing is possible. The whistle-blower's attorney demonstrates why I thought so, in a letter to the acting director of national intelligence, Joseph Maguire:

> The purpose of this letter is to formally notify you of serious concerns we have regarding our client's personal safety. We appreciate your office's support thus far to activate appropriate resources to ensure their safety.
>
> The events of the past week have heightened our concerns that our client's identity will be disclosed publicly and that, as a result, our client will be put in harm's way. On September 26, 2019, the President of the United States said the following:
>
> **I want to know who's the person that gave the Whistleblower, who's the person that gave the Whistleblower the information, because that's close to a spy. You know what we used to do in the old days when we were smart? Right? With spies and treason, right? We used to handle them a little differently than we do now.**
>
> The fact that the President's statement was directed to "the person that gave the Whistleblower the information" does nothing to assuage our concerns for our client's safety. Moreover, certain individuals have issued a $50,000 "bounty" for "any information" relating to our client's identity. Unfortunately, we expect this situation to worsen, and to become even more dangerous for our client and any other whistleblowers, as Congress seeks to investigate this matter.[38]

Four days later, Trump said his team "was trying to find out" the whistle-blower's identity.[39]

A day after that, he wondered in a tweet, "why aren't we entitled to interview & learn everything about . . . . the Whistleblower, and also the person who gave all of the false information to him"?[40]

There's a great line—the subheadline, actually—of a story in the now-shuttered *Pacific Standard* magazine, about Trump and cult behavior.

"What do you call an organization where total loyalty to a charismatic but volatile leader is strictly enforced?" it asks.[41] I'll let you guess the word.

And I'll show you once more that word in action— congressional Republicans rallied to Trump's defense over the Ukrainian mess en masse. Sure, some of them grumbled off the record, according to one House Democrat.[42] And few of them were alarmed or even critical on the record, though they were among the more independently minded "usual suspects," such as senators Lisa Murkowski and Mitt Romney.[43] But far more of them were there again to man the front lines on Trump's behalf, in the face of evidence and reason. That includes the two highest-ranking Republicans in Congress, Senate majority leader Mitch McConnell and House minority leader Kevin McCarthy. It also includes the House Republicans' number two, Steve Scalise, who went back and forth with George Stephanopoulos during a November 2019 interview after he was asked for his response to Deputy Secretary of State John Sullivan's comment that "[s]oliciting investigations into a domestic political opponent, I don't think that would be in accord with our values."

Scalise: Well, first of all, that's not what was happening on the phone call. Even when the president said will you do me a favor, he then went on to ask about Crowdstrike, that wasn't about Joe Biden. And so taking that out of context . . .

Stephanopoulos: No, it's about his domestic political opponents. And the transcript clearly shows the president was asking the Ukrainian president to investigate his political opponents, both the Democrats in 2016, Joe Biden going forward. Do you think that was appropriate?

Scalise: That wasn't, first of all, about political opponents. The law, George, requires President Trump, or any president, when they're sending foreign aid, taxpayer money, to another country, to ensure that that country is rooting out corruption. He and [Ukrainian president] Zelensky were talking about that on the phone call.

Stephanopoulos: The only two instances he raised were Crowdstrike in 2016, involving the Democrats, Burisma in 2017 and '18 involving Joe Biden. And again, it's just a very simple question, do you think it's appropriate for the president to ask the Ukrainians or the Chinese, which he's also done in public, to investigate his domestic political opponents?

Scalise: Well, first of all on that call he was not talking about the 2020 election or political opponents, he was talking about corruption relating to the 2016 elections.

Stephanopoulos: That's not what the transcript shows.[44]

Trump critics on the right are often accused of being part of some club that's out of touch with reality. When the "reality" is built upon "alternative facts," I guess I have no choice but to confess.

Chapter 6

THE NARCISSIST

It'd be impossible for you to picture the earth by looking at just your backyard. Sure, you could describe what you see, and what you see would certainly be a part of some bigger image. But the planet is so vast, so varied, so colorful that you'd have to pull way, way, way back to take in all of its roundness and its blue and its green. And withdrawing to that point takes time. The same goes for grasping Donald Trump's total mental unfitness for office—the real and obvious instability in his conduct that Americans witness every day. There is an overwhelming number of examples, only a few of which have been chronicled in this book so far. They can't be judged as though they're one-offs, because ultimately, they're more like individual brushstrokes on some yuge mural. In sum, they add up to an overwhelming and worrying picture no one could possibly appreciate by staring at it up close—by thinking about Trump twenty-four hours in a row.

There's no way to succinctly describe all the occasions long before he got into politics that Donald Trump called reporters on the phone pretending to be his own spokesman—not as a gag but as a serious disguise—so he could defend his business deals or brag about his romantic life.[1] There's no way to briefly recall all the instances when he has denied saying or doing things that he *said on the record*, with evidence to back it, or *did in plain sight*, with cameras and witnesses around. If I tried to put the full evidence of Trump's megalomania into words here—I mean, it'd take a thousand pages, and the pages would spontaneously combust. (And people would say they'd never seen anything like it, believe me.)

So instead of doing any of that, I'd like to recognize a couple of people who've already tried. George Conway and Peter Wehner are loyal conservatives—loyal to principle, not to some guy who holds some political title—who've explained Trump's behavioral dangers at length and why they're *the* reasons, above any others, to oppose him as president. Wehner, who was a speechwriter and policy adviser for President George W. Bush and served in the Bush 41 and Reagan administrations before that, made that point pretty much from day one. Pay attention to the italicized part of the following quote, which comes from an interview he did with C-SPAN in July 2016: "I think [Trump] is temperamentally unfit to be president. I think he's erratic, I think he's unprincipled, I think he's unstable, and I think that he has a personality disorder; I think he's obsessive. And at the end of the day, having served in the White House for seven years in three administrations and worked for three presidents, one closely, and read a lot of history, *I think the main requirement to be President of the United States isn't where you check the boxes on policy, though I think policy is very important . . . but it is temperament, it's disposition, it's the idea of whether you have wisdom, and judgment, and prudence.*" (My emphasis.)[2]

Peter's description of the presidency is dead on. The job of president isn't to own the libs or the conservatives. It isn't to be a culture warrior, to purge every frustration about politics and society we've ever had—and that goes for the Republicans who can't stand the media and Hollywood the same as it does for the Democrats who condescend to middle America. The job of president is to oversee the world's most powerful government and to use that power measuredly in most cases, appropriately in the most stressful ones, and intelligently in all of them. Let me tell you: *Donald Trump's extreme narcissism prevents him from doing any of that.*

As Conway noted in an essay in *The Atlantic*, our Founding Fathers made it so that the president would be a "public fiduciary," whose fundamental responsibility was to do what was best for the country. "To act as a fiduciary requires you to put someone else's interests above your own, and Trump's personality makes it impossible for him to do that. No president before him, at least in recent memory, has ever displayed such obsessive self-regard. For Trump, Trump always comes first. He places his interests over everyone else's—including those of the nation whose laws he swore to faithfully execute. That's not consistent with the duties of the president, whether considered from the standpoint of constitutional law or psychology."[3]

The psychology angle on Trump has gotten a lot of airtime and column space the last few years. Conway himself has argued that Trump's conduct meets the literal book definition of something called "narcissistic personality disorder," which the *Diagnostic and Statistical Manual of Mental Disorders (DSM)*—the authoritative guide for health professionals on such things—says is evidenced by a set of nine criteria, any five of which need to be present for there to be a diagnosis. Whether mental health professionals would diagnose Trump with this condition is a discussion exclusively for them. But that discussion is irrelevant to deciding whether the president's mentality causes him to fail in his office and fail the nation. Conway and Wehner have made the points respectively that you don't need to be a doctor to tell that a football player suffered a gruesome leg injury or be a mechanic to tell that your car is leaking oil and puffing smoke from underneath the hood. I think reasonable people should agree that one, mental health is a serious topic, and two, we can treat it with the sensitivity it deserves while observing something pertinent about our country's chief executive: that he acts like a destructive egomaniac any way you look at it.

I'd like to look at it from the perspective that Trump lacks sound judgment to a large extent exactly *because* he's a narcissist. It impairs his ability or his willingness—your guess is as good as mine—to make good choices in his capacity as president, regardless of whether those choices are about policy or simply enforcing laws as he is constitutionally bound to do. The problem is that Trump's narcissism makes him mistrust any advice that goes against his own instincts and his self-described "great and unmatched wisdom."[4] Only somebody omnipotent could get away with dismissing *everything* but his own mind and experience—every set of data, every expert insight, every alternative—and come to the best conclusion every time. Trump, although he'd never admit it, is not omnipotent. So he needs to rely on outside sources to guide his decision making, even when he has a strong instinct one way or the other.

Of course, that's not his style. As he told the *Washington Post* in an interview, "I have a gut, and my gut tells me more sometimes than anybody else's brain can ever tell me."[5]

I know, I know—that's the rebellious, screw-the-Poindexters attitude that many of the people who voted for him liked, especially after eight years of a president who prided himself on being cerebral and cosmopolitan, while leaving half of Americans feeling as though they had been cast off as dumbass bumpkins. But people: Don't. Buy. The. Sham. Donald Trump is not the commonsense cowboy he thinks he is. Give this paragraph from Conway—which is fully cited—a chance:

> In July [2019], [Trump] described himself in a tweet as "so great looking and smart, a true Stable Genius!" . . . That "stable genius" self-description is one that Trump has repeated over and over again—even though he has trouble with spelling, doesn't know the difference between a hyphen and an apostrophe, doesn't appear to understand fractions, needs basic geography lessons, speaks at the level of a fourth grader, and engages in "serial misuse of public language" and "cannot write sentences," and even though members of his own administration have variously considered him to be a "moron," an "idiot," a "dope," "dumb as shit," and a person with the intelligence of a "kindergartener" or a "fifth or sixth grader" or an "11-year-old child."[6]

I should pause here to say that just because Trump has demonstrated these characteristics and his subordinates have described him this harshly doesn't mean I view his supporters the same way. Because I absolutely do not. I made that point in the opening chapter, but it bears repeating here: Trump has *conned* people into believing he's a big deal by talking a big game— truly bigger than anyone in US politics has ever talked it. If you were a voter fed up in 2016 with the political status quo—a Bush here, a Clinton there, Romney, Obama, not one of them, in your opinion, stopping the country from going in a direction you didn't like—you might have asked yourself, why not believe Trump's bluster? After all, his name is on *everything*, it seems. He's been one of America's most famous celebrities since the 1990s. He had that TV show with a catchphrase *everyone* used all joshing-like for years. "Trump" seems like a successful brand and a successful man. If he says he wants to do the same for the country and do it by speaking the language of the average Joe for once—instead of talking about how some trade deal would be awesome for our "GDP" and our "economic growth," talk about what it may do to *my* community and *me*—why in the hell wouldn't I give him the chance?

That's why it's so important to acknowledge that *two* things can be true: one, Trump is right that politicians have lost touch with common Americans, and two, he is the wrong man to look out for them. Because when the going gets tough, he will *look out only for himself.* He cares about the concerns of flyover country only as long as seeming to care gives him power. If he *truly* cared—if he were an actual problem solver—then wouldn't he use every tool at his disposal to make the United States' problems go away? Yes, he would. But he doesn't. Here's what he does, instead, to quote Conway once more:

> Trump claims to be an expert—the world's greatest—in anything and everything. As one video mash-up shows, Trump has at various times claimed—in all seriousness— *that no one knows more than he does about: taxes, income, construction, campaign finance, drones, technology, infrastructure, work visas, the Islamic State, "things" generally, environmental-impact statements, Facebook, renewable energy, polls, courts, steelworkers, golf, banks, trade, nuclear weapons, tax law, lawsuits, currency devaluation, money, "the system," debt, and politicians.* (My emphasis.)[7]

This is a new level of megalomania. He's completely dismissed the possibility that *anyone* knows more than he does about this stuff. And I honestly think that if you listen to the guy talk for a few minutes *without* thinking about what political party he belongs to—yours or someone else's—you'd have a difficult time concluding that he wasn't epically narcissistic about his brilliance and capacities. Good leaders understand that they're not the smartest person in the room sometimes, even a lot of the time. Donald Trump implies that he has intelligence on the scale of a fucking *god*. It is *ludicrous*. And we have to take him at his word that he really believes it. If Trump were just joking, he wouldn't back up his supposed supergenius by *acting* as though he were a supergenius—as though he knew better than the weathermen, because Dorian was truly threatening Alabama, and so he had the hurricane map drawn on to prove it. (Here again, you can see how several chapters in this book can apply to single episodes of his behavior.)

Let me pose the same question here that I did about Trump and his cult: *Okay, so why does it matter?* I'll acknowledge that talking about all of his awful traits isn't revealing any startling new insight into the president's nonexistent character. Everybody, even most of his fans, knows what sort of person he is. Trump's personal favorability is in the tank; tons of his voters, in surveys and in conversations, don't defend his personality; only the most burn-it-down of his backers actually like the fact that Trump talks to dictators as though they met on a dating app and has zero self-control on Twitter. The problem is, many of his fans think it doesn't matter. Here are two reasons why it does.

One: all these categories of kinglike or authoritarian actions eventually cause a society to collapse if you let them go on long enough, and two: a clear-as-day character defect such as narcissism prevents Trump from delivering on many of the promises he makes.

Trump's narcissism influences or even controls his decision making and then produces conclusions and follow-through that are bad for the United States. Because we don't have all day, I'll take just a few examples to show you what I mean.

One, which applies more to the dystopian societal collapse business, has to do with how Trump mistakes himself, as president, for "the state." What do I mean? Let's take the instance of Adam Schiff, the California Democrat and chairman of the House Intelligence Committee, exaggerating a transcript of a call between Trump and the Ukrainian president, Zelensky, in September 2019. During a committee hearing, Schiff mischaracterized Trump's side of the exchange like this: "It reads like a classic organized crime shakedown. Shorn of its rambling character and in not so many words, this is the essence of what the president communicates: *We've been very good to your country, very good. No other country has done as much as we have. But you know what? I don't see much reciprocity here. I hear what you want. I have a favor I want from you though. And I'm going to say this only seven times so you better listen good.*" (My emphasis.)[8]

He went on like that for a minute before bookending his "this is the essence" caveat with "This is in sum and character what the president was trying to communicate with the president of Ukraine." Whether it actually *was* what he was trying to communicate hadn't been formally investigated at the time—but from Trump's perspective, it wasn't.

Now, if you're a hard-core Trump supporter, you probably absolutely *loathe* Schiff—and even if you're a garden-variety Republican, an independent, or (believe it or not) a journalist, you're likely to be skeptical of his conduct in some way.

George Stephanopoulos, the former Bill Clinton aide turned ABC News host, asked Schiff during his weekly Sunday program why he would "make up dialog for dramatic effect, even if it's a parody, as you say?"[9] I mention that to make clear that I'm not about to defend Schiff. Rather, I want to show how Trump's reaction to Schiff demonstrates his delusions of grandeur. First, there was this tweet:

> Rep. Adam Schiff illegally made up a FAKE & terrible statement, pretended it to be mine as the most important part of my call to the Ukrainian President, and read it aloud to Congress and the American people. It bore NO relationship to what I said on the call. Arrest for Treason?[10]

There you have it: the president of the United States just casually wondering if federal law enforcement should arrest the House Intelligence Committee chair and charge him with a crime punishable by death. "Well, maybe he was just joking," one might say. Well, here Trump is later that week speaking to press in the Oval Office:

> The whistleblower started this whole thing by writing a report on the conversation I had with the president of Ukraine. The conversation was *perfect*, it couldn't have been nicer. I saw [Senator] Rick Scott, I saw many of the senators talking about it, many of the congressmen talking about it—not a thing wrong. Unless you heard the Adam Schiff version, where he made up my conversation. He actually made it up. It should be criminal, *it should be treasonous*. He made it up, every word of it, made up,

and read it to Congress as though I said it. And I'll tell you what, he should be forced to resign from Congress, Adam Schiff. He's a lowlife. He should be forced to resign. He took a *perfect* conversation, realized he couldn't read it to Congress, because it was *perfect*—it was a very nice conversation. I knew many people were on the phone. Not only were many people on the phone, we had stenographers on the phone taking it down word for word. He took that conversation—*which was perfect*—he said, I can't read this. So, he made up a conversation and reported it and said it to Congress and the American people. And it was horrible, what he said. And that was supposed to be coming from me. But it was all fabricated. He should resign from office in disgrace, and frankly, *they should look at him for treason*, because he is making up the words of the President of the United States. (My emphasis.)[11]

He called a conversation "perfect" four times, which was weird enough. (Have you ever heard someone use that word to describe a damn phone call?) But he also described Schiff's actions as "treasonous" and, to make sure there was no misunderstanding, said Schiff should be "looked at"—meaning investigated—"for treason." Now, I want you to read the federal statute that spells out the consequences for being guilty of treason. Pay special attention to what—not who—the object of treason is in this language from the US Code:

Whoever, owing allegiance to the United States, levies war against them or adheres to their enemies, giving them aid and comfort within the United States or elsewhere, is guilty of treason and shall suffer death, or shall be imprisoned not less than five years and fined under this title but not less than $10,000; and shall be incapable of holding any office under the United States.

Whoever "levies war against" . . . the United States.
Whoever "adheres to [the] enemies" of . . . the United States.
Whoever gives "aid and comfort" to the enemies of . . . the United States.
Treason is a crime of acting against *the nation*.

Leave aside for a moment the fact that nothing Adam Schiff did was—my word, I can't believe I actually have to say this—actually "treasonous." He embellished, overstated, what have you, the president's portion of a call transcript with a foreign leader, and he qualified it twice by saying that the embellishment or overstatement was what he read between the lines. The issue relevant to Trump's narcissism is that he believes this was an offense committed against *the nation*. In effect, Trump is saying that treason is a crime that attacks not the United States but Donald Trump. When another politician mischaracterizes Donald Trump, it is *treason*. He said that. And his words carry weight because he's the president.

This is so nuts, so manipulative, so self-obsessed, so megalomaniacal that I don't know where to begin, because there are so many places to do it. I guess I may as well start here: "treason" is not a word you bandy about when you're the president. Look, I understand that Trump has cheapened the meaning of words—and our politics in general was already devaluing them before he came along. A progressive nonprofit called the Action Project released an ad in 2012 that showed an actor playing House Speaker Paul Ryan wheeling "granny" off a cliff—to criticize his position on Medicare reform.[12] For years, Republicans called Barack Obama a socialist—a word we've gained a new appreciation for in the era of politicians such as Bernie Sanders. I confess that as a talk radio host, I was part of the trend of using hyperbole to criticize public figures and government policies I disagreed with. But I can't underscore this enough: there is a massive difference between a person who *is not* the president of the United States using exaggerated political language and a person who *is* the president of the United States saying, adamantly and repeatedly, that somebody inside the Department of Justice should "look at" one of his political opponents for the heinous act of treason just for exaggerating a comment that was *clearly* made for dramatic effect. If we can't agree on that—if we can't say that the nation's chief executive directly accusing a member of the other party of *that* crime is a bridge far, far too far—then we can't ever screw the lid back on. Because what will happen is that we will normalize presidents explicitly saying that someone on the other side of the aisle should possibly face death over something as minor as a rhetorical dispute, until one of those presidents is *just crazy enough* to get DOJ to try the case.

And just in case this seems like an isolated incident, the previous week Trump made a similar charge against the person who spoke to the whistle-blower who had uncovered the Zelensky phone call. "Whoever the hell they saw—they're almost a spy," he said at a private event. ". . . Who's the person who gave the whistleblower information? Because that's close to a spy. You know what we used to do in the old days when we were smart? Right? The spies and treason, we used to handle it a little differently than we do now."[13]

Back in February 2018, Trump took issue with Democrats

who refused to clap at his State of the Union address. He blustered that they were "Un-American. Somebody said treasonous. I mean, yeah, I guess, why not? Can we call that treason? Why not?"[14]

Remember something I highlighted in a previous chapter about the president abusing his power: he does not see a line between himself and the Justice Department, which is supposed to make prosecutorial decisions independent of his suggestions and free of White House interference. He bullied his first attorney general for not opening investigations he wanted opened—and that AG, Jeff Sessions, was eventually pushed out.

He said the Time Warner–AT&T merger shouldn't happen—and the Department of Justice filed suit to block it.

He said his Democratic rival Adam Schiff should be brought up on treason charges. What will happen next?

Folks, can we not mess around with this one? Okay? Can we not? Because it's a little too scary. It's a little too like the totalitarian governments that sanction the murder of political dissenters. Let's not get even 5 percent of the way to that. Let's not even *begin* down that path. Let's remember what our nation is *not*, which is a nation that exhibits even a morsel of the habits of Kim Jong-un and his barbaric forerunners. Let's put a stop to this right now and say that Donald Trump doesn't belong within a thousand miles of the type of power he threatens to use casually, all because someone hurt his feelings.

That, my friend . . . is why this matters. Rhetoric has consequences.

And then, as covered earlier, there's Trump's delusion that he's the world's foremost expert ever on virtually everything. This one flows straight from the second excerpt of Conway's essay, in which he names all the subject areas that Trump says he knows more about than anyone else. Literally anyone else. If the president believes he knows better than anyone else how to handle the likes of Kim and Xi and Putin, how to set the country's trade policy, how to fix our leaky southern border and immigration policy generally, and how to eliminate the national debt—then what information do you think will inform his decisions? Going back to the quote from a few paragraphs ago: "I have a gut, and my gut tells me more sometimes than anybody else's brain can ever tell me."

When you're drunk on your own superiority like this, you'll reason that you can do anything, because the rules don't apply to you. We've seen this with Trump and the rules of arithmetic and economics. There are also rules—even informal ones, or what are called "norms"—covering the president's comportment in office. I want to highlight one of them here, in the context of his narcissism: not selling out your country for your personal political gain, of which there are all too many examples. One is Trump's phone call with Zelensky the morning of July 25, 2019, which reads at some junctures like standard, diplomatic sucking up—and then some. "We worked a lot" to win an election, Zelensky said, "but I would like to confess to you that I had an opportunity to learn from you." And then: "Well yes, to tell you the truth, we are trying to work hard because we wanted to drain the swamp here in our country." I guess the Ukrainian leader really takes the marketing advice "Know your audience" to heart.

But other parts of the call weren't so funny. At one point, Zelensky said his government was "almost ready to buy more Javelins [missiles] from the United States"; Trump responded right after by saying "I would like you to do us a favor, though," which was when he went into this conspiracy theory stuff about a server being housed in Ukraine and how Zelensky's government should work with Attorney General William Barr to investigate it. Zelensky responded approvingly: "Yes it is very important for me and everything that you just mentioned earlier. For me as a President, it is very important and we are open for any future cooperation. . . . I also plan to surround myself with great people and in addition to that investigation, I guarantee as the President of Ukraine that all the investigations will be done openly and candidly. That I can assure you."

Then Trump continued, "Good because I heard you had a prosecutor who was very good and he was shut down and that's really unfair. A lot of people are talking about that, the way they shut your very good prosecutor down and you had some very bad people involved. . . . The other thing, [t]here's a lot of talk about Biden's son, that Biden stopped the prosecution and a lot of people want to find out about that so whatever you can do with the Attorney General would be great. Biden went around bragging that he stopped the prosecution so if you can look into it. . . . It sounds horrible to me."[15]

Then there was the interview he did with Stephanopoulos about a month and a half before the Zelensky call:

Stephanopoulos: Your campaign this time around, if foreigners, if Russia, if China, if someone else offers you information on opponents, should they accept it or should they call the FBI?
Trump: I think maybe you do both. I think you might want to listen, I don't, there's nothing wrong with listening. If somebody called from a country, Norway, "We have information on your opponent." Oh, I think I'd want to hear it.

Stephanopoulos: You want that kind of interference in our elections?

Trump: It's not an interference, they have information. I think I'd take it. If I thought there was something wrong, I'd go maybe to the FBI. If I thought there was something wrong. But when somebody comes up with oppo research, right, that they come up with oppo research. Oh, let's call the FBI. The FBI doesn't have enough agents to take care of it, but you go and talk honestly to congressmen, they all do it, they always have. And that's the way it is. It's called oppo research.[16]

Then there was what Trump said on the White House lawn in October amid the Ukraine mess. He was critical of business dealings involving companies associated with Hunter Biden, the former vice president's son, and China: "China should start an investigation into the Bidens, because what happened in China is just about as bad as what happened with Ukraine."[17]

Those are two clear-cut examples of Trump asking a foreign government to investigate his political opponent—sandwiching his admission that he'd accept dirt from a foreign government on a political opponent—in the span of three and a half months. He does it because he thinks he can get away with it. When he says, "I have an Article II, where I have the right to do whatever I want as president," it's fair to interpret him pretty broadly.

In writing about how the United States elects its presidents in *The Federalist Papers, No. 68*, "The Mode of Electing the President," Alexander Hamilton stated this: "Nothing was more to be desired than that every practicable obstacle should be opposed to cabal, intrigue, and corruption. These most deadly adversaries of republican government might naturally have been expected to make their approaches from more than one quarter, but chiefly from the desire in foreign powers to gain an improper ascendant in our councils. How could they better gratify this, than by raising a creature of their own to the chief magistracy of the Union?"

That's not quite so straightforward—the language is a little outdated for how we communicate today. But the point is this: it is vital that foreign governments do not influence our presidential elections. Trump asks for this influence directly—he did it in 2016 from Russia, he did it in 2019 from Ukraine and China, and he's extended an open invitation to anyone else, because to him, it's just "oppo research."

He thinks he knows better than anyone else the basic definitions of a "trade deficit" and a "budget deficit." He thinks he knows better than the economists' consensus about trade: Harvard economist N. Gregory Mankiw, who left the Republican Party in October 2019 partly because of Trump, wrote that "[e]conomists are famous for disagreeing with one another, and indeed, seminars in economics departments are known for their vociferous debate. But economists reach near unanimity on some topics, including international trade." That consensus, according to a letter to congressional leaders from Mankiw and thirteen other economists who have led the President's Council of Economic Advisers, is that "[i]nternational trade is fundamentally good for the U.S. economy, beneficial to American families over time, and consonant with our domestic priorities."[18] But as unintelligent as these two things are, they do not actively betray the public trust. Trump thinks he knows better than Alexander Hamilton—than the no-brainer that another nation should not be a player in a presidential election.

That, Mr. President, is "traitorous." And politics be damned, it's impeachable on principle.

Chapter 7

FIXING THE PRESIDENCY

The greatest danger that Donald Trump poses to this country domestically isn't about tariffs, as bad as I think those are. It's not about the national debt, as much as I care about that, and it's not about the wall, as much as I think the country needs one. It's about something that goes beyond how we look at the world from either "the right" or "the left." It's about *Trump himself*: his unfitness, his dishonesty, his disloyalty, his cruelty, his incompetence, his narcissism, and a whole host of other adjectives I'll spare you so I don't belabor the point. In January 2017, someone took over the office of president *only to begin destroying it*—with his personality, which bends to no laws or rules, and his self-interest, which directly conflicts with the president's job to do what's right for the country instead of himself. It's now up to us to set aside our political differences and take the well-being of our democracy into our own hands.

I get that this isn't the sexiest thing in the world. It's not the red-team-versus-blue-team type of problem that we're used to shouting about on Twitter or a cable news panel. But please trust me on this one: we won't *have* a United States of America if we let the presidency permanently turn into a gig for narcissistic charlatans who don't give a damn about the Constitution, norms, and tradition. What good will Congress be if the president ignores the laws it passes or goes around it to, in effect, make his own? What's the point of draining the swamp if the president will just refill it using any means necessary? How will the public be able to trust the president at all if he looks out only for himself? How will our allies? And how will our adversaries use it to their advantage?

It was evident before Trump that the presidency wasn't perfect or invulnerable. Hell, just look at what Richard Nixon did during Watergate. In the same way we moved on from that era, Congress, the American people, and future presidents *themselves* have to pledge to shoring up the weaknesses in the office that Trump has exposed. It's the only way we can make sure that our nation's chief executive is answerable to the public and the other branches of government; to make sure that we aren't elevating strongmen by a different name. In this country, we don't elect kings. And we need to make sure that we have the laws and the universal commitment to "take care that the laws be faithfully executed."

If you aren't convinced of how essential this is to the United States' health, let's think about how the shoe always seems to find its way to the other foot in politics. Do you remember when President Obama created the Deferred Action for Childhood Arrivals (DACA) program without the instruction of Congress? Holy hell, did Republicans—including myself—throw a fit. I remember when the media got after us for holding Obama's feet to the fire and how affronted we were because of it. Going back to my old House colleague Mick Mulvaney, a fellow Tea Partier, who said it like this, according to reporter Tim Alberta: "When we do it against a Republican president [instead], maybe people will see it was a principled objection in the first place."[1] Mick was spot on. But now that Trump is president—and Mick is his chief of staff—the same Republicans who wouldn't let Obama do whatever he wanted with his powers are letting Trump run wild. My party is no longer made up of defenders of the law but instead apologists for a president who abuses it. Just look at how Congress let Trump's emergency declaration on the border go through, despite the principled and admirable objection of a handful of lawmakers on my side of the aisle. I'm here to tell you: if your reason for letting that stand is that "the Democrats would do the same to thing to us," then just wait to see what the Democrats will actually do. Wait until a Democratic president declares a national emergency of gun violence and creates new restrictions on firearms without Congress's sanction. Wait until that person makes the Green New Deal official policy because of a climate emergency. You don't have to imagine all that much, since Democratic politicians have already telegraphed their interest in such an approach.[2] Here's the thing about mutually assured destruction: it's supposed to be a *deterrent*, not an incentive to go bombs away on the other guy.

So let's look at the job of president through the lens of something other than conservatism and progressivism. Let's look at it like ordinary, commonsense people who value our democracy and the rule of law, and let's oppose people who would erode those foundations.

What would such a group stand for? What would it believe?

Well, first, it would believe that anyone running for president or occupying the Oval Office should not do *anything* that only an authoritarian would do. Only an authoritarian would use disinformation to sow doubt among the public about reality.

Trump, whose administration has admitted to peddling "alternative facts," pushes conspiracy theories, and then has the gall to treat the mainstream press as "fake," does this all the time. Chillingly, this continuous campaign of lying has trickled its way down the government ranks. In October 2019, a Customs and Border Protection (CBP) officer asked a journalist from the website Defense One if he wrote propaganda *four times* before the man, news editor Ben Watson, relented, said yes, "[f]or the purposes of expediting this conversation," and was handed back his passport.[3] As Defense One noted, many other journalists have been harassed by CBP at ports of entry during the Trump administration.

Authoritarians use their perches to threaten individuals or businesses that they don't like personally, whether for political reasons, personal beefs, or any other conceivable excuse that doesn't fall under the purview of law enforcement. Trump has done this with respect to the AT&T–Time Warner merger (the resulting entity of which owns CNN) and Amazon CEO Jeff Bezos (who owns the *Washington Post*).[4] He's done it by browbeating individual reporters whose coverage rubs him the wrong way. This sort of conduct is bullying, plain and simple. And it's enabled by the extraordinary influence of the presidency.

Authoritarians believe in and practice one-man rule—so they ignore the legislative process if it's inconvenient to them. The perfect example is the national emergency on the southern border.

They find dubious ways to install lackeys in Senate-confirmable positions without the Senate's consent.

They whip up mobs to intimidate political opponents and government institutions.

In short, they run afoul of or undermine the Constitution,

federal law, and other instruments of democracy. They insist that you ignore the evidence right in front of your face and instead accept their version of the "real world," in which they are perfect and the individuals and institutions trying to hold them accountable are dangers or phonies. They go it alone—and snooker people into following them down a dark path. That word, "authoritarian," might sound a little academic, I know—so let these examples give you an idea of what I mean. America has no business allowing such a person to be in charge of it.

Donald Trump is the first US president in modern times to provide an example of this kind of autocrat. He's a menace to our form of government. And he should not be emulated; rather, his style of rule should be rejected outright.

Though that's primarily a matter of presidents policing their own behavior, there are things Congress can do to formalize how it oversees the office. And given Trump's presidency, it should. The current administration is a walking billboard for the need to curb abuses of executive power. Take the example of the national emergency on the southern border. Contrary to popular belief, the Constitution does not give the president authority to declare one. Rather, under the National Emergencies Act, the president may use powers delegated by Congress to declare the existence of a national emergency and invoke the authority to do certain things under law, such as take money that Congress has appropriated for a certain military construction purpose and use it for a different one. That happened with the border situation: the Pentagon allowed $3.6 billion worth of funds dedicated to such entities as a middle school on an army base, warehouses for hazardous materials, and firing ranges to be diverted to building the border wall.[5] Now, I don't think that should be allowed to stand—there's no emergency to construct a big ol' border barrier. (More on the specifics of that later.) But in general, the president's authority under the National Emergencies Act doesn't give him the ability to go around the process of legislating whenever he wants to. And that needs to be made clear by lawmakers. One option is the ARTICLE ONE Act from Utah Republican Senator Mike Lee, a strongly bipartisan bill that would make future emergencies declared under the NEA expire after thirty days, unless Congress votes to extend them.[6]

Congress could also deter the kind of interference Trump has committed through the Justice Department that we've seen on certain antitrust cases. There's nothing wrong with presidents setting law enforcement *priorities*. But law enforcement *decisions* about whether to prosecute a case and how prosecutors should proceed once a decision is made should be based on the facts and the law, period. The president's preferences and priorities ought not to be involved. Historically, the White House has ensured that the Oval Office kept its distance from DOJ. The White House Counsel's Office typically releases guidance at the beginning of a new administration outlining what kind of contact between the White House and Justice is appropriate and what isn't. Trump's administration is no exception, in fact; former White House counsel Don McGahn sent such a memo to all White House staff just a week after the inauguration.[7] But this kind of language is informal and relies on a "scout's honor" sort of arrangement to be upheld. It's obvious that we need stronger protections on the books to ensure the independence of Justice Department law enforcement actions. Congress should approve legislation to mandate transparency of communication between the White House and the Justice

Department to give the American people assurances that law enforcement is operating free of political interference.

There's also the issue of Trump going around the Senate to fill some of his cabinet posts. As I wrote earlier, the president controversially relied on a sort of "next man up" arrangement to make Matthew Whitaker former attorney general Jeff Sessions's replacement; his administration created a new position inside the Department of Homeland Security from whole cloth to use that same theory to make Ken Cuccinelli the acting director of citizenship and immigration services. But although Trump has abused some permissions of the Federal Vacancies Reform Act (FVRA) to achieve this, he's not the first president to do so. During the previous administration, President Obama skirted the law to place people into powerful positions without going through the Senate confirmation process. One example is the case of Vanita Gupta, who served as Obama's acting assistant attorney general for more than two years, longer than the FVRA allowed her to.[8] This kind of circumvention or outright abuse of the system fundamentally undermines our system of checks and balances; it empowers the executive branch to ram through political appointees who would otherwise not make it through Senate confirmation. Congress should fix the gaps in FVRA that allow this, so that the Senate's advice-and-consent role doesn't become optional.

Then there are the abuses of power related to the Mueller investigation. I know, I know—the president's team has tried to make it fake news, old news, or no news at all since the special counsel first began looking into Russia's interference in the 2016 election. But the ways Trump obstructed—yes, obstructed—that probe call for a response from Congress beyond just oversight and impeachment proceedings. There's a need for legislation. Take the way the president dangled pardons for Michael Cohen and Paul Manafort in exchange for their not cooperating with Mueller. That fundamental misuse of the pardon power—potentially invoking it to save his own ass—is not exactly what the Founding Fathers had in mind when they wrote Article II of the Constitution. The pardon is a means by which to correct past wrongs, extend mercy to the deserving, and generally correct for politically motivated missteps. President Obama's pardon of nonviolent drug offenders facing mandatory sentence minimums, for instance, was a perfect example of a worthy presidential pardon; likewise, President Trump's pardon of certain incarcerated Americans such as Alice Marie Johnson is laudable. Congress should make clear its opinion that offering a pardon in return for obstructing justice or intentionally undermining the law—as Trump has reportedly thought about doing for officials who violate statutes to get the southern wall built—is unconstitutional. Lawmakers should also pass a bill beefing up congressional oversight of the process and making it more transparent, including requiring the executive branch to turn over materials relevant to a pardon that was issued for corrupt or self-protective reasons.

Related to this, presidents cannot be allowed to obstruct the workings of justice, such as a DOJ investigation. In my opinion, the laws already on the books about obstruction of justice absolutely apply to a president's abuse of his official powers. It's a general principle that criminal laws apply to everybody—including the president and those close to him, including his advisers and aides. This is common sense to most Americans, because we believe in the rule of law, not of men—and therefore no man is above the law. But there's been some disagreement about this statement within the Justice Department's own ranks, based on a legal memo from the Office of Legal Counsel stating that a president cannot be indicted while in office. Mueller invoked that precedent when he declined to make a prosecutorial decision about the evidence of Trump's obstructive behavior—instead he simply said that he could not exonerate the president of such an offense. Given these complications, I support Congress approving legislation reaffirming that obstruction-of-justice statutes apply to the president—making clear that the Department of Justice cannot immunize presidents from facing accountability for the crime.

Beyond that, I think we need protections for special prosecutors who are appointed to investigate allegations of executive-branch wrongdoing. I certainly hope that the United States won't need more of these kinds of investigations in the future. But when they're warranted and they proceed, they need to be able to move forward independently, without presidents exerting their influence on what are supposed to be impartial proceedings. It's simple fairness: if somebody is under investigation for having committed a crime, he doesn't get to fire the prosecutor to get himself out of trouble. That applies to the president of the United States, too. Though it's true that the president sits atop the food chain and can either appoint or remove certain senior executive-branch officials, he can't do it for corrupt purposes. Trump's interference with the Mueller probe, including his efforts to fire Mueller, have revealed cracks in the existing guardrails against political interference in high-profile investigations. The appropriate response is legislation reaffirming that the president cannot fire or interfere with the work of a special counsel, FBI director, attorney general, or any other law enforcement official for purposes of ending an investigation that involves him, his campaign, his family, or his business interests.

I wish this kind of norm didn't need to become a law; it's a sign that presidents can't be trusted to call their own fouls and need a referee. But it's both appropriate and legal. Congress has the authority to enact criminal statutes to protect the integrity of congressional, grand jury, and judicial proceedings against obstructive acts by any person, including the president. The Constitution requires the president to "take care that the laws be faithfully executed," prohibiting presidential action taken in bad faith—for instance, obstruction of justice. A president who obstructs justice not only is violating the law, he is violating the Constitution.

Trump has had a difficult time—or just hasn't cared about—disentangling his duty as president from conflicts of interest and outside influence, whether financial or governmental (or both). The most egregious—and impeachable—examples concern his soliciting the help of foreign states to win an election. In front of a microphone, for all the world to hear, he invited Russia's help in 2016: "I will tell you this, Russia: If you're listening, I hope you're able to find the 30,000 emails [of Democratic opponent Hillary Clinton] that are missing."[9] He asked Ukraine for help in 2019 under the false pretense that Ukraine's former prosecutor general had stopped an investigation into a company that employed Hunter Biden at Joe Biden's urging: "There's a lot of talk about Biden's son, that Biden stopped the prosecution and a lot of people want to find out about that so whatever you can do with the Attorney General [William Barr] would be great. Biden went around bragging that he stopped the prosecution so if you can look into it. . . . It sounds horrible to me."[10]

He said with reference to China, "China should start an investigation into the Bidens, because what happened in China is just about as bad as what happened with Ukraine."[11]

And he said he'd welcome that kind of assistance from anyone, Russia, Ukraine, China, or otherwise: "If somebody called from a country, Norway, 'We have information on your opponent.' Oh, I think I'd want to hear it. . . . It's not an interference, they have information. I think I'd take it."[12] Trump is actually *devoted* to using the help of foreign governments to win election. He's either too stupid to understand why this is wrong or doesn't care that it is. Either way, this is another situation requiring an answer from Congress. We must do everything we can to prevent what Alexander Hamilton called "foreign powers . . . gain[ing] an improper ascendant in our councils." Lawmakers should take additional steps to make sure that any offers of illegal foreign assistance are made public and promptly reported to the appropriate authorities, including the Federal Election Commission and the Federal Bureau of Investigation.

All of that relates directly to abusing the system for his political interests; then there's doing so to advance his financial interests. Recall the emoluments examples from a previous chapter: federal officials frequenting Trump properties and hosting events there and Trump himself directing official White House visits to Trump-branded locales and proposing that the next meeting of G7 nations take place at the Trump National Doral Miami golf resort in Florida (the last of which, thankfully, he backed away from after facing significant public pressure).[13] That's a big fat no-no. Congress should make a law requiring presidents—and, perhaps, all federal lawmakers—to divest from significant business holdings or, where feasible, put them into blind trusts.

That's not the only family business of note. The American people must have confidence that the president is acting first and foremost in the interest of the public, not in the personal interest of himself or his family members. Yet the Trump family has been an integral—and official—component of the Trump presidency. All White Houses, including this one, should be held to the standards set out in the "Bobby Kennedy law": "A public official may not appoint, employ, promote, advance, or advocate for appointment, employment, promotion, or advancement, in or to a civilian position in the agency in which he is serving or over which he exercises jurisdiction or control any individual who is a relative of the public official."[14] Moreover, Congress should pass legislation clarifying that antinepotism laws apply to the White House, a move well within its constitutional authority.

All of the preceding detail in this chapter is . . . well, it's a lot. It's a sign that Donald Trump has turned the presidency into something it shouldn't be: a job with unlimited ability to advance one's own personal interests at the expense of the public's. That's a damn shame. One of the coolest things about our federal government—and maybe the one I value most—is that our Founders went out of their way to create an "energetic" executive that was still beholden to the people. "There is hardly any part of the system which could have been attended with greater difficulty in the arrangement of it than this," Hamilton wrote about designing the presidency in *The Federalist Papers, No. 69*, "The Real Character of the Executive." For a world that didn't have much experience with rulers who *weren't* monarchs or tyrants, it was a hell of a thing to write up plans for a president who would be strong—but not too strong. Here is Hamilton describing the difference:

The President of the United States would be an officer elected by the people for FOUR years; the king of Great Britain is a perpetual and HEREDITARY prince. The one would be amenable to personal punishment and disgrace; the person of the other is sacred and inviolable. The one would have a QUALIFIED negative upon the acts of the legislative body; the other has an ABSOLUTE negative. The one would have a right to command the military and naval forces of the nation; the other, in addition to this right, possesses that of DECLARING war, and of RAISING and REGULATING fleets and armies by his own authority. The one would have a concurrent power with a branch of the legislature in the formation of treaties; the other is the SOLE POSSESSOR of the power of making treaties. The one would have a like concurrent authority in appointing to offices; the other is the sole author of all appointments. The one can confer no privileges whatever; the other can make denizens of aliens, noblemen of commoners; can erect corporations with all the rights incident to corporate bodies. The one can prescribe no rules concerning the commerce or currency of the nation; the other is in several respects the arbiter of commerce, and in this capacity can establish markets and fairs, can regulate weights and measures, can lay embargoes for a limited time, can coin money, can authorize or prohibit the circulation of foreign coin. The one has no particle of spiritual jurisdiction; the other is the supreme head and governor of the national church! What answer shall we give to those who would persuade us that things so unlike resemble each other? The same that ought to be given to those who tell us that a government, the whole power of which would be in the hands of the elective and periodical servants of the people, is an aristocracy, a monarchy, and a despotism.

For most of US history, presidents have fit the description of them that Hamilton laid out. Trump has not. Let's go line by line. He has joked repeatedly about being "a perpetual," as Hamilton put it, saying after Xi Jinping made himself president for life, "I think it's great. Maybe we'll have to give that a shot someday."[15] Not only has Trump not been "amenable to personal punishment and disgrace," he's continually evaded both. Kings have "an absolute negative" of the acts of the legislature, Hamilton wrote, whereas presidents do not—but that's not how Trump sees the president's emergency powers. Presidents have a "concurrent authority in appointing to offices" with the Senate, you say? Trump has trampled on the part of that responsibility shared with the Senate to help surround himself with bootlickers. And not to put too fine a point on it, but presidents are supposed to possess "no particle of spiritual jurisdiction." Yet Trump favorably quoted from a conspiracy theorist a comment that "the Jewish people in Israel love him . . . like he's the King of Israel. They love him like he is the second coming of God."[16] Trump himself one day looked to the heavens and said "I am the Chosen One"[17]—apparently sent to Earth to make the United States' commerce with China fairer.

We've been told by Trump supporters over and over again not to take him so literally about such things, since they're likely to be asides or jokes. In certain circumstances, that's probably true. But Trump has not earned the right to be trusted in such a way. He may not really think he's a literal godsend. He may not really believe that Article II of the Constitution gives him the right to do "whatever I want." But when he behaves in an unhinged manner around the clock, it's difficult to imagine him regarding himself as anything less than a supreme leader, who is immune from the rules and regulations that check everyone else in society. All men and women of good conscience who care about seeing our democracy through to the next generation *have* to do everything in our power to make sure someone like Trump can't get away with such conduct. If we don't, it'll be our undoing. And no number of conservative judges will be able to stop it.

Chapter 8

FIXING CONSERVATISM

Until about January 20, 2017, the term "Republican in name only" (RINO) described members of the GOP who wavered on the party platform. I'll admit that the goalposts of that "platform" moved depending on the day; what counted as a conservative position one moment could be insufficiently conservative the next (such as when Republicans fought for Obamacare repeal). But in general, you were a RINO if you were a Republican member of Congress who voted for bloated spending deals, "open borders," or legislation that betrayed a core right-of-center principle. The point is that the label had at least *something* to do with government policy.

As of January 21 that year, the test for being a RINO shrank to one question: Do you pledge your undying support to our king, or don't you? I wish I were exaggerating. But there's no exaggerating the force of a cult's pull. Let's remember what Trump said during the 2016 campaign: "I could stand in the middle of Fifth Avenue and shoot somebody, and I wouldn't lose any voters."[1] Truly, I want to spend a minute taking that possibility seriously. We tend to grimly accept his comment at face value without diving into what "not losing any voters" would actually look like, what contortions are necessary to make Trump committing a crime, to put it in simpler and more realistic words—say, obstructing justice!—come off as defensible behavior. *This*, my friends, is how we truly uncover the way Trump has bastardized conservatism. Because each time he has trashed norms and tested legal limits, he's been putting the spirit of his Fifth Avenue theory into practice. Each of these actions on the Trump agenda has required dismissing yet another principle—and these precedents have become scaly barnacles glomming onto the rotting hull that is conservative politics.

I don't want to give goofy-ass grifters more attention than they deserve—which is literally any—but there's a Trump sycophant named Bill Mitchell who hosts an internet radio show whose tagline is "Trust Trump." Those two words speak volumes about the direction of conservatism under this president. It's about following Trump wherever he goes. If he goes *there* . . . well, it's always a matter of his having the chutzpah to go *there* like previous swampy politicians didn't. If he asks foreign powers to investigate his political opponents . . . well, the Biden family *does* seem shady, right? If he's investigated by his own government for his campaign's connections to Russia doing something along those very lines . . . well, it's that traitorous deep state again! If journalists dig into his own shady connections and pretty obvious financial conflicts of interest . . . well, it's that enemy of the people, the fake news, again! I swear to you, "conservatism" under Trump looks like a fucking conga line. It's all about putting your hands on the shoulders of the flunky ahead of you and shuffling your feet forward, wherever the procession leads. And because that is the state of affairs—because conservatism means whatever Trump needs it to—

being a conservative often isn't about anything related to what we call the usual "public discourse."

Under Trump, bullying political opponents is conservative.

Under Trump, pressuring the Department of Justice to impede the business of adversarial media is conservative.

Under Trump, hanging a picture of the president and his North Korean BFF Kim Jong-un on a wall in the West Wing—seriously, the White House staff did that—is conservative.[2]

Under Trump, having zero skepticism of the president—the pinnacle of authority in our political system—and instead accepting his "great and unmatched wisdom" is conservative.[3]

Of course, there's nothing remotely conservative about any of these things, since conservatism is, among other things, about restraint, obedience of law, and trust in experience, not in whims. But "conservative" has a pretty all-encompassing definition right now; it's satisfied only if you defend the whole Trump package. That's evident when it comes to the personal conduct and the abuse of powers described above—but it also applies to the substance.

Under Trump, going around Congress to get money for a border wall, like sneaking into Mommy's vanity drawer for forty bucks, is conservative.

Under Trump, overseeing an increase in the national debt of $3 trillion is conservative, because no one really cares about the national debt.

Under Trump, ethnonationalism—finding new ways to reject refugees, to dehumanize immigrants of color, to undermine Ronald Reagan's vision that any law-abiding foreigner could come to the United States and become an American—is conservative.

Conservatives should remember that these failings bear no

resemblance to what it is to be a conservative at all. In fact, some of them are representative of quite the opposite. Former Republican senator Judd Gregg of New Hampshire put it this way:

> It is difficult to know what the president's philosophy is.
>
> It changes constantly, with the only constant being his self-indulgence.
>
> A strong case could be made that he has no ideological consistency; his erratic purposes and inconsistent courses would make a weathervane appear steady.
>
> He has had numerous epithets attached to him by his opponents and by some of the former members of his administration.
>
> But here is one that has not been mentioned yet: The president seems to have a definite tinge of socialism in his chaotic policy closet.[4]

If you think about it, being an ardent protectionist on trade, trying to tell companies which countries they can do business with, letting it rip on the budget, and browbeating the Federal Reserve into making our dollar weaker—"a policy that has deep roots in the socialist movement that has always been a part of the Democratic Party's policy matrix, starting with William Jennings Bryan more than a century ago . . . [and] has been a minority position even within the Democratic Party," Gregg wrote—is kinda socialist. Now, does that make Trump a socialist with a capital S? It does not. There's a lot more to Trump: his views on the tax system, the federal government's role in health care, and immigration are anathema to the left wing. But if you mix all of this gobbledygook together, it's tough to get the sense that Trump has a guiding set of principles at all—beyond enhancing his own power, of course. I think we've seen enough to conclude that he doesn't have a core idea in his body. Bear in mind that:

- At first, Trump was registered as a Republican (1987–1999); then he became a member of the Independence Party (1999–2001); then he became a Democrat (2001–2009); then he became a Republican again (2009–2011); then he became an independent (2011–2012); then he became a Republican a third time (2012–today).[5]
- He proposed a $6 trillion tax hike when he was flirting with running for president on the Reform Party ticket in 2000.[6]
- He described himself as "very pro-choice" and said he wouldn't ban partial-birth abortion in 1999, and he was all over the place on the issue in 2016 after coming around to the pro-life position.[7]
- He called "[o]ur $17T national debt and $1T yearly budget deficits . . . a national security risk of the highest order" in 2012. As president, he's helped enable the national debt to balloon to $23 trillion.[8]
- He criticized President Obama for "negotiating with our sworn enemy the Taliban—who facilitated 9/11."[9] He invited Taliban leaders to Camp David for a meeting in 2019.[10]
- And his views on what was impeachable behavior have—well—evolved over the years. "Are you allowed to impeach a president for gross incompetence?" he tweeted in 2014.[11]

Trump is all over the place in these examples, flipping from right to left or left to right. This amply backs my belief that Gregg shares and articulated: "[H]e does not have any core policies, just those ideas that he happens to stumble onto while watching some late night talk show. So it is not possible to hang a title on him that claims he is this or that."[12] I'd add one thing: It's not possible to do it *credibly*. The great conservative leader Phyllis Schlafly's final book before her passing, *The Conservative Case for Trump*, argued that Trump "could be the most conservative and successful president since Ronald Reagan."[13]

Trump has tried claiming the label himself. "Remember when I first started running? Because I wasn't a politician, fortunately. But do you remember I started running and people would say, 'Are you sure he's a conservative?' I think now we've proved that I'm a conservative, right?" he told the Conservative Political Action Conference in 2018.[14]

Well . . . is he wrong? Because he *did* appoint Supreme Court justices Neil Gorsuch and Brett Kavanaugh. He *did* sign an enormous tax cut package into law. He *has* undone some of the previous administration's regulatory regime. How can these achievements be called anything but "conservative" successes? Look—they are. But they're fortunate successes, not part of some brilliant conservative master plan. For every major right-of-center vow he's kept, he's broken or completely ignored another. He's made deficit spending worse than it was when Obama left office. He's not overseen the construction of the wall; as of fall 2019, he'd just managed to replace some existing old fence with new fence and build a little new barrier, but not of the "big and beautiful" variety. He totally botched the repeal and replacement of Obamacare, contributing absolutely no knowledge or leadership to the process. Instead of improving the United States' trade policy overall, he's screwed it up to the point that his administration has had to bail out farmers with taxpayer money. That is why it's significant that Trump isn't a conservative—because ultimately *you can't trust him* to deliver conservative victories. The ones that he's provided seem more like happy accidents than the products of design.

Think about it this way: if Trump changed his position on issues *a, b, c,* and *d* yesterday, he could change his position on issues *e, f, g,* and *h* tomorrow—or change his position on issues *a, b, c,* and *d* again. His legacy of "flip-flopping" is much more comprehensive than the norm in politics, such as Mitt Romney's becoming pro-life and John Kerry's "I actually did vote for the $87 billion before I voted against it" gaffe. Those are single instances of wavering. Trump has shifted his views about *a lot* of things *a lot* of times. It's because there's no "there" there. Trying to get him to explain his stances on matters important to conservatives is like asking a fifth grader to stand in front of the class and work a calculus problem on the blackboard. He's totally out of his depth. That's a *gigantic* liability as president, because, as the old belief in DC goes, it takes presidential leadership to make major reforms. For example, it would've been awfully helpful to have a president who was at least somewhat interested in federal health care policy taking charge during the Obamacare battles in 2017. Republicans didn't have one of those.

Trump *claims* that they did, naturally. "Nobody is more negative on ObamaCare than Donald Trump. . . . And nobody knows health care better than Donald Trump," he told George Stephanopoulos before the Iowa caucuses in 2016.[15] But as with so many issues, he couldn't back up his claim; he could back it up barely a fraction. He had one talking point about Obamacare reform: allowing individuals to purchase insurance across state lines, which we can call "getting rid of the lines" for shorthand. Here's how he employed it in a debate shortly after the Stephanopoulos interview:

Question: OK, so let's talk about pre-existing conditions. What the insurance companies say is that the only way that they can cover people is to have a mandate requiring everybody purchase health insurance. Are they wrong?

Trump: I think they're wrong 100 percent. What we need— look, the insurance companies take care of the politicians. The insurance companies get what they want. We should have gotten rid of the lines around each state so we can have real competition.

We thought that was gone, we thought those lines were going to be gone, so something happened at the last moment where Obamacare got approved, and all of that was thrown out the window.

The reason is some of the people in the audience are insurance people, and insurance lobbyists, and special interests. They got—I'm not going to point to these gentlemen, of course, they're part of the problem. . . .

But, we should have gotten rid of the borders, we should have gotten rid of the lines around the state[s] so there's great competition. The insurance companies are making a fortune on every single thing they do.

I'm self-funding my campaign. I'm the only one in either party self-funding my campaign. I'm going to do what's right. We have to get rid of the lines around the states so that there's serious, serious competition.

Question: But, Mr. Trump . . .

Trump: . . . And, you're going to see—excuse me. You're going to see preexisting conditions and everything else be part of it, but the price will be done, and the insurance companies can pay. Right now they're making a fortune.

Question: But, just to be specific here, what you're saying is getting rid of the barriers between states, that is going to solve the problem. . . .

Trump: That's going to solve the problem.[16]

This is almost incoherent. The question wasn't terribly clear, but the point is that Obamacare had a provision nicknamed the "individual mandate" that required Americans to have medical insurance or pay a monetary penalty to the government. The question that was posed to Trump is whether the federal government's having that kind of mandate in law was necessary for insurance companies to be able to afford covering every American shopping for a plan. Trump's answer, roughly, was no, because the government could allow consumers to shop for insurance across state lines, which would create "great" and "serious" competition. I guess the argument is that competition would lower the price of insurance, making it affordable to more individuals, which would entice more individuals to purchase a policy, making the individual mandate unnecessary. I don't buy for a second that Trump could make this argument if he was asked, "How *exactly* would 'getting rid of the lines' solve the problem?" But although it's an interesting idea on the merits, it's just one isolated idea about an issue that needs a lot of them. It's like saying that your plan to win a war is to send a carrier group to *xyz* coordinates. Okay, that's possibly a good step and we should talk more about it, but what else? Is that it?

Florida senator Marco Rubio, one of Trump's Republican competitors in 2016, picked up on that point and exposed Trump's ignorance. "Here's what you didn't hear in that answer, and this is important guys, this is an important thing. What is your plan?" he asked Trump directly. "I understand the lines around the state, whatever that means. This is not a game where you draw maps. . . . What is your plan, Mr. Trump? What is your plan on healthcare? You don't have a plan." Trump's response consisted mostly of insults: "I watched [Rubio] melt down two weeks ago with Chris Christie" and "I watched him repeat himself five times four weeks ago. . . . I watched him meltdown on the stage like that, I've never seen it in anybody. . . . I thought he came out of the swimming pool." The only meat in his reply to Rubio was "You get rid of the lines, it brings in competition. So, instead of having one insurance company taking care of New York, or Texas, you'll have many. They'll compete, and it'll be a beautiful thing."

"Alright. So, that's the only part of the plan? Just the lines?" Rubio asked.

"The nice part of the plan—you'll have many different plans. You'll have competition, you'll have so many different plans," Trump answered.

The exchange was enough for the moderator to press Trump for more: "If you could talk a little bit more about your plan. . . . Can you be a little specific . . ."

"There is going to be competition among all of the states, and the insurance companies. They're going to have many, many different plans," Trump replied.

"Is there anything else you would like to add to that . . ."

"No, there's nothing to add. What is to add?"[17]

Well, there is a ton to add, because conservative policy scholars have labored over creating an alternative to Obamacare for years. Trump was incapable of saying even "Look, there's more to this, but I think the lines are the biggest part of it and they're what I think is important to focus on tonight." The best he could do was ask, "What is to add?"—because obviously he was genuinely unaware that there was anything more to consider.

Is it any surprise that barely a month after being inaugurated, when the GOP led off its legislative agenda with health care reform, Trump said, "Now, I have to tell you, it's an unbelievably complex subject. Nobody knew health care could be so complicated."[18] Is it any surprise that Republicans wound up proposing options that most of the public despised? And is it any surprise that more than a year after they failed, Trump still vowed, "The Republican Party will become 'The Party of Healthcare!'"[19]—and Rubio said, after meeting with the president about the subject, "He didn't offer a plan"?[20] It's poetic, I tell ya.

So here's the bottom line about Donald Trump and his politics: he has no core philosophy; the north star he follows is whatever delivers him power or allows him to keep it; his platform is built around indulging his supporters' cultural grievances instead of solving their problems; any overlap he has with conservative beliefs is incidental; and those last two things make him an unreliable champion of conservativism and the people he supposedly represents. This will be especially important for the years 2021 through 2024—because if he doesn't have to worry about satisfying his voter base anymore, he's liable to act unleashed. How can we trust him to govern like a conservative—which includes honoring the rule of law—if he'll never have to face the electorate again? The answer: we can't.

One of the core components of being conservative is being consistent. Donald Trump is as erratic and undependable a leader as this nation has ever had.

Both conservatives and the United States in general deserve better. We need to start putting our faith in ideas instead of people again. Blind partisanship means we end up voting for any man with an R next to his name, no matter how degraded or moronic he is. And this partisanship is one consequence of the Trump cult. The Republican Party is the United

States' conservative party, yet it has sold its soul to a man who is demonstrably not conservative. The Republican Party has historically comprised many factions—people such as Reagan, Pat Buchanan, Bob Dole, George W. Bush, Rand Paul, and Trump-like "populists" such as Rick Santorum all under the same roof—which ultimately benefits the exchange of ideas. It's an iron-sharpens-iron sort of thing. But not only has the GOP determined that Trump is the best of what this competition has produced; it has concluded that his is the only acceptable opinion. Dissent from within the party by people like me is quashed by party leaders, as if I'm no different from a Democrat. (Spoiler alert: I'm very different.) The healthy thing for people on my side of the aisle to do is to advocate strongly for conservative causes. The unhealthy thing to do is to vouch single-mindedly for a man who has selectively adopted a handful of them at the expense of trampling on the rule of law we claim to hold dear. That seems awfully shortsighted—a short-term gambit by a group of people who usually judge the world by long-term stakes.

As this book has argued, those long-term stakes are just, oh, the well-being of maintaining our democracy and resisting the ever-increasing threat of something resembling dictatorship. If you believe that appointing Gorsuch and Kavanaugh, putting through a tax cut, providing some relief from regulation of the private sector, and just generally keeping the libs at bay is worth empowering China and Russia at our expense, running an almost completely cowardly foreign policy, shafting our farmers, wasting the best opportunity to move on from Obamacare, and exploding the debt, you're a glass-half-full type of Trump supporter. If you believe that all those wins outweigh the losses— and *also* the most damaging parts of this presidency, which were detailed in the previous chapters of this book—then I'd argue that we're looking at a deal with the Devil. "What he brings is the manner, the lying, the name-calling, all of this, which I think will do more lasting damage to the country—you can't unring these bells—than Nixon's surreptitious burglaries did," the archconservative columnist George Will said.[21] As Trump has shown, presidents can change the tax policy and regulations and foreign policy stance of previous administrations. But enabling rule by cult, the justification of government with disinformation, and the serial abuse of executive power— the hallmarks of authoritarianism that the United States has gone to war against throughout its history—can be really tough to undo. You can't whip people into a frenzy and then bring in someone who will calm everything down in a snap.

Being conservative is all about being judicious. We conservatives need to reintroduce that temperament into US politics. It'll make all of us more stable—and saner.

We also need some consistency in a conservative agenda. As I wrote at the beginning of this book, I absolutely believe that Donald Trump touched a nerve with some of his policy proposals, not just his attitude. (Even if the attitude was most of his shtick.) The federal government ought to do a better job— any job at all, really, since it hasn't tried much—of helping set up our working class for success. That means, for once, thinking about how the policies of today will affect the generations of tomorrow. To quote Will again: "We used to borrow money for the future—we fought wars for the future, built roads, harbors, airports for the future—now we're borrowing from the future to finance our own consumption of government goods and services, and everyone's agreed on this. It seems to me the political class is more united by self-class interest than it is divided by ideology in this regard."[22]

As Trump discussed during the 2016 campaign, the nation

could use some better roads and harbors and airports, since so many of them are in a state of disrepair and we've neglected them for too long. But as Trump *didn't* discuss, we also need to shore up the accounts for federal retirement benefits (which I'll discuss later). The actuaries have said for years that Social Security and Medicare are headed for insolvency. Reaching that point would be a disaster. And not to fix them would be to ignore, selfishly, the well-being of our youngest generations and future generations as we move forward in the twenty-first century.

If we want to have a policy debate about how technology will affect the public's future, we need to make sure we're doing it within the constraints of the Constitution. I swear, of all the disruption that tech has caused and will continue to cause Americans, Twitter and Facebook enforcing their community standards is *waaaay* down the list of priorities; in fact, I'm not even sure it's *on* the list. Sure, Twitter and Facebook have a left-of-center bias. But they're private companies. They can have whatever rules and resulting biases that they want. Everybody has a right to call them out for it and boycott their services— but there is no role for government here. Government should stay out. The true threats technology presents are in things such as cyberwarfare, AI, and automation. Research by the Brookings Institution[23] found that more than 70 percent of the tasks in industrial production, food service, and transportation are susceptible to being automated—that's blue-collar work such as molding and casting, operating chemical plants and the machines inside the plants, truck driving, and construction. It's not just China that may put these people out of business; it's tech. So how do we want to react to it to make sure that our economy can accommodate people who will need to work in new industries? These are the kinds of topics that need to be at the core of conservative discussions.

And when we look abroad, we need to remember that the world is better off when the United States is helping lead it. We can't cede moral authority in the twenty-first century to the likes of China, a Communist state of systematic censorship and oppression, and Russia, so long as the thuggish Putin or a strongman like him remains in charge. There's a lot of gray area between saying "The United States is not the world's policeman" and saying that the United States ought to be everything to all people. Going entirely the first way is how the United States hastily abandoned its Kurdish partners in northern Syria to slaughter by Turkey and risked setting ISIS fighters back on the loose. I appreciate President Trump's desire to keep the men and women of our military at home. I think that's a thoughtful instinct and forces us to reckon with the toll of armed conflict. We should incorporate it into our foreign policy—while remembering that the cost of not taking every last measure to ensure that ISIS remains locked up before getting out of the area is reintroducing a threat to innocent Americans on our own soil. I'll say it again: part of being conservative is trusting in experience. By Trump's own admission, he'd rather trust his assumptions and not be questioned.

The United States needs a strong, coherent center-right party to help guide it through this rapidly changing world. We don't have that right now. We have a weak center-right party because of its members who are too afraid to speak truth to authority and too willing to exchange foundational principles for short-term power. All we have to do to break away from this lapse in judgment is reprioritize the integrity of our minds above the gut of one man.

Chapter 9

FIXING THE DEBT

As you may have figured out by now, I think it's far more serious that Donald Trump has damaged the institutions and instruments of our democracy—the Constitution and the law, the free press and fact-based debate, the presidency itself and the national character—than that he has botched some government policies that the country prioritizes in more "normal" political times. But that doesn't make such outcomes irrelevant. As an economic conservative, I'm steamed that Washington has allowed the national debt to grow out of control and that the Trump administration is turning our economy into an example of "bad ideas from the nineteenth century" that you'd find in a college textbook. As a border hawk, I feel completely let down about the president's unfulfilled pledge to get a handle on illegal immigration and build a wall. This goes without mentioning a couple of issues that *could* present crises for the nation: our lack of planning for how to deal with climate change and the near-term explosion in the number of retirees, which contributes to the debt threat. These unresolved problems are what make the Trump era a double whammy. Not only has the political world had to prioritize protecting our democracy, but doing so has come at the expense of working on the challenges we were already letting get out of hand.

I want to discuss a few of these of particular interest to conservatives—the federal government's deficit spending and debt, the United States' new and costly approach to international trade, and the wall—from a particular perspective. These matters are complicated enough already without taking into consideration how qualified our public officials are to act effectively upon them. But Trump has raised the degree of difficulty by one big-ass order of magnitude. I think you can connect his character defects, which are examined in the bulk of this book, *directly* to his abject failure to restore fiscal sanity in DC, maximize the benefit of exchanging goods and services worldwide, and rein in illegal immigration as a competent (and preferably compassionate) adult would do.

Let's begin with the debt—and revisit this beauty from an interview Trump did with the *Washington Post* during the 2016 campaign:

> **Trump:** We've got to get rid of the $19 trillion in debt.
> **Bob Woodward:** How long would that take?
> **Trump:** I think I could do it fairly quickly, because of the fact the numbers. . . .
> **Woodward:** What's fairly quickly?
> **Trump:** Well, I would say over a period of eight years. And I'll tell you why.
> **Woodward:** Would you ever be open to tax increases as part of that, to solve the problem?
> **Trump:** I don't think I'll need to. The power is trade. Our deals are so bad.
> **Woodward:** That would be $2 trillion a year.

Trump: No, but I'm renegotiating all of our deals, Bob. The big trade deals that we're doing so badly on. With China, $505 billion this year in trade. We're losing with everybody. And a lot of those deals—a lot of people say, how could the politicians be so stupid? It's not that they're stupid. It's that they're controlled by lobbyists and special interests who want those deals to be made.[1]

Okay. There are really two parts to his pledge.

The first part is that he would eliminate all of the federal debt in eight years. Though that's simply unrealistic for any president to accomplish, it could be chalked up to typical overpromising by a presidential candidate. He walked the statement back some in a subsequent interview, saying that the government could pay off some undefined percentage of the debt over a decade—not all of it—"depend[ing] on how aggressive you want to be."[2] But how firmly he pledged to do something about the United States' red ink isn't the issue here.

The issue is the second part: that the country could pay off untold trillions of dollars of debt by making NAFTA more effective and doing the same with the United States' other trade pacts. Notice how he said that it would be a direct and preferable alternative to raising taxes. "I don't think I'll need to. The power is trade. Our deals are so bad. . . . The big trade deals that we're doing so badly on. With China, $505 billion this year in trade. We're losing with everybody."[3] As the saying goes, that's not how any of this works. Yes, it didn't seem 100 percent certain that Trump was saying that the money we're "losing" in trade with China and other countries could somehow be used to pay down the debt. But read what he said across the table from South Korean president Moon Jae-in in 2017, a handful of months after he was inaugurated: "The United States has trade deficits with many, many countries, and we cannot allow that to continue. And we'll start with South Korea right now. But we cannot allow that to continue. This is really a statement that I make about all trade. For many, many years, the United States has suffered through a massive trade deficit. That's why we have $20 trillion in debt."[4]

That, ladies and gentlemen, is Donald Trump saying the United States is in debt because it imports more than it exports. That is so moronic—so mind-numbingly dumb—that it's insulting: insulting to conservatives who care about fiscal responsibility; insulting to Wharton graduates who actually know what the hell they're talking about; insulting to the public, which counts on the president to make choices on its behalf that are informed by sound data and reasoning. One of the most basic prerequisites of doing that is understanding rudimentary economics. Trump doesn't.

Thankfully, the folks at the bipartisan nonprofit Committee for a Responsible Federal Budget are more patient than I am. They explain:

> Years of budget deficits have accumulated into the national debt, currently $19.8 trillion.* Yet the budget deficit is determined by the tax and spending decisions made by Congress and signed into law by the President, regardless of how much American consumers and businesses buy from other countries.
>
> In a thought experiment, let's pretend that every good and service purchased in the United States this year was

---

*That was as of the time of writing, July 6, 2017.

produced here. There would be no trade deficit. But most federal spending would be unchanged—the size of government agencies and the military, the amount of Social Security and Medicare benefits, the amount of veterans' and retirement benefits, etc. Federal revenues, which are driven mainly by the structure of income and payroll taxes and the total amount of income in the economy, would also be similar. If spending and revenue don't significantly change, neither will budget deficits.

To be sure, the trade and budget deficits are somewhat related to each other. *But the cause-and-effect is largely the opposite of what President Trump suggests.* It isn't that higher trade deficits lead to higher budget deficits, but rather [that] higher budget deficits tend to indirectly lead to higher trade deficits. Currently, about $6 trillion, or a little less than one-third of the gross debt, is currently held by foreign countries and investors. Higher budget deficits can result in more foreign-held debt which in turn can impact the trade deficit (another one-quarter of the gross debt is money the government owes itself and does not have even an indirect relationship with trade deficits.) (My emphasis.)[5]

As George Conway noted, one of the knowledge areas in which Trump graded himself as the smartest of anyone in the world is "trade."

Trump is bullshitting you.

And there's no reason he shouldn't be able to play it straight. As the president of the United States, he has around him some folks who are pretty smart about these things. His first chairman of the Council of Economic Advisers was Kevin Hassett, who advised every Republican nominee for president dating back to George W. Bush in the year 2000 and has been an economics professor and a member of the Federal Reserve board of governors. His second, Tomas Philipson, is a world-renowned economist from the University of Chicago. His first budget director, Mick Mulvaney, who is now his chief of staff, is also no dummy. He was a strict fiscal conservative when I served with him in the House; he called the first budget President Obama proposed during his tenure in Congress "a joke," adding "It's hard to explain how detached from reality this is, to think that the country can spend another $1.6 trillion when it doesn't have the means. It means either you haven't been paying attention or you don't care."[6] Long story short: Trump has the experts he needs to get him up to speed.

Instead, he stubbornly has the United States in reverse. Only an obstinate narcissist who thinks he knows better than anyone else could possibly misunderstand so severely how the federal budget works.

There's more evidence than just his comment to President Moon to support criticizing Trump's lack of knowledge. One of the more jaw-dropping ones is his belief about mandatory federal spending—most of which is often called "entitlement spending"—on Social Security and Medicare. Trump has consistently held that he could save Social Security—which faces big shortfalls in the future (more on that in a minute)—just by taking care of inefficiency and misspent money in the program. "I'm the only one who is going to save Social Security, believe me," he said during a Republican primary debate in February 2016. The moderator pressed him: "OK. But how would you actually do that? Can I ask you? . . ."

"Because you have tremendous waste," he said. "I'll tell you." . . .

"You have tremendous waste, fraud and abuse. That we're taking care of. That we're taking care of. It's tremendous. We have in Social Security right now thousands and thousands of people that are over 106 years old. Now, you know they don't exist. They don't exist. There's tremendous waste, fraud and abuse, and we're going to get it. But we're not going to hurt the people who have been paying into Social Security their whole life and then all of a sudden they're supposed to get less. We're bringing our jobs back. We're going to make our economy great again."[7]

To unpack this: Trump believes that removing the deceased from benefit rolls and "taking care" of other administrative errors will keep Social Security solvent in the long run—and also that the job market and economy will improve under his watch. Which, I guess, will boost payroll tax payments, which fund Social Security, to the point that the program will *definitely* be all set.

In what is a recurring theme for him, he's living in an alternate universe on this one. Social Security is the single most expensive federal program by a long shot. In fiscal year 2018 (the period between October 2017 and September 2018), it accounted for $982 billion, or about a quarter of all spending. Budget experts often measure Social Security expenditures as a share of gross domestic product (GDP)—a way of seeing how government is growing relative to the economy. In FY 2018, taxpayer dollars spent on Social Security were equal to about 4.9 percent of GDP. Put a pin in those numbers for a sec.

Because the baby boomer generation is hitting retirement age in droves, the cost of the benefits the government will owe retirees is about to explode—so much so that by the year 2020 it will exceed the total money the Treasury takes in to cover it. (Most of that money is payroll tax collections.) Now, Social Security does have reserves—but the program will have to start dipping into them to account for the yearly expenses of the program. The Social Security Board of Trustees projects that those reserves will be exhausted by the year 2035.[8] After that, all the tax income of the program will be enough to pay only about three-quarters of the benefits for the following half century–plus—meaning that people born around 1970 or earlier will get short shrift. In the year 2036, it will be people born around 1971. The bottom line is that people who today are under the age of fifty aren't expected to receive even one year of the full benefits the government is obligated to provide them— unless it begins to make some legitimate changes.

Trump thinks the necessary changes are (1) getting rid of "waste, fraud, and abuse" and (2) essentially "growing" our way out of the problem—creating such a humming economy that a bajillion Americans have jobs and pay payroll taxes. This, my friends, is not a realistic way to close the gap. First, the Social Security trustees already bake into their report what they think the United States' future employment situation will look like. They, like most reasonable people, do not expect that the United States will soon have a labor market twice its current size, able to foot the bill for Social Security with extra payroll tax receipts. It's *literally impossible*. Second, remember the statistics I asked you to put a pin into a couple of paragraphs ago? In FY 2018, our GDP was about $20.5 trillion,[9] and the dollar cost of Social Security equaled about 4.9 percent of that. In FY 2039, the Congressional Budget Office projects, GDP will be $45.7 trillion—and the Social Security trustees project that Social Security's expense will equal 5.9 percent of *that*. In other words, over the next two decades, Social Security is projected to grow faster than our overall economy.

So you tell me: is the reason for that cost growth "waste, fraud, and abuse"? No. It's the fact that a tidal wave of people is going to hit retirement soon! Jeez. This is not that hard.

We absolutely should root out misspending in Social Security, just as we should across the whole federal government. But to believe that doing so will magically get the government back into the black is delusional—or willfully misleading. In early 2019, *The Daily Beast* reported this:

> Since the 2016 presidential campaign, Donald Trump's aides and advisers have tried to convince him of the importance of tackling the national debt.
>
> Sources close to the president say he has repeatedly shrugged it off, implying that he doesn't have to worry about the money owed to America's creditors—currently about $21 trillion—because he won't be around to shoulder the blame when it becomes even more untenable.
>
> The friction came to a head in early 2017 when senior officials offered Trump charts and graphics laying out the numbers and showing a "hockey stick" spike in the national debt in the not-too-distant future. In response, Trump noted that the data suggested the debt would reach a critical mass only after his possible second term in office.
>
> "Yeah, but I won't be here," the president bluntly said, according to a source who was in the room when Trump made this comment during discussions on the debt.[10]

Well, well, well, what a selfless man! Clearly putting the long-term financial health of the United States is at the very center of his agenda.

There have been and will be people close to Trump who say, "Oh, no, no, he really cares, just you wait and see." Those people can shut it and stop insulting my and everyone else's intelligence. Trump doesn't give *one. single. shit.* It's because ignoring the United States' looming entitlement and debt crises is best for him politically. Sure, Trump is not the first politician, including many members of Congress, to make this calculation. But it sounds as though he's in rare company just admitting it. He is not a public fiduciary. Instead, he's selfish. He's a narcissist.

If we actually want to fix Social Security for people of retirement age fifteen years from now and beyond, we have to make the numbers work using math, not a magic wand. The Committee for a Responsible Federal Budget has an outstanding tool on its website that shows how much money certain reforms to the program would cost or save.[11] These are some of the options for savings we have to choose from: raising the retirement age, slowing the percentage growth of benefits for everyone or those of certain earners by income level, changing how the government calculates inflation, raising how much of a person's earnings are payroll taxable, raising payroll tax rates, and means-testing benefits for high-earning seniors. You may be thinking, *Man, all of those sound pretty icky.* But you know what? That's how it goes when the bills come due. For all the bitching that Republican politicians have done over the years about running the government like a business, you'd think every CEO in the private sector had spent his or her company's money like there was no tomorrow.

But, hey—if you believe the economic advisers close to Trump, *that's exactly how he prefers to manage your tax dollars.*

I don't want to give short shrift to Medicare, because the

government spends about as much on it as on our defense budget. It's actually forecasted to be relatively more expensive than Social Security in the long run: Medicare will overtake Social Security by 2040 and be about 5 to 7 percent costlier over the subsequent fifty years, per the Social Security and Medicare trustees. The part of it that's backed by payroll taxes, Medicare Part A—which pays for inpatient hospital services, skilled nursing facility and home health care services following hospital stays, and hospice care—will no longer have any reserves by 2029. After that, Part A will be able to cover only 77 to 89 percent of costs over the next sixty-five years. The part of it that isn't backed by payroll taxes, Medicare Parts B and D—which help pay for physician, outpatient hospital care, home health care, and other services for individuals who have voluntarily enrolled—is funded mostly out of general tax revenue. Because of that, beneficiaries of Parts B and D don't face the same risk of benefit cuts as a result of inadequate financing. "However," the trustees predict, "the aging population and rising health care costs cause SMI [supplementary medical insurance] projected costs to grow steadily from 2.1 percent of GDP in 2018 to approximately 3.7 percent of GDP in 2038."[12] About three-quarters of that increase—hundreds of billions of dollars—will have to come from somewhere in the federal budget.

My questions are: From where? Do we increase taxes on individuals, corporations, certain goods and services, or some combination of those? Do we get the money from other federal programs? What happens when angry voters, powerful business interests, and the advocates of the other programs that stand to lose money to fund Medicare begin to protest and threaten lawmakers with grassroots campaigns and advertising opposing their reelection? Do the lawmakers give in and pass the buck—or the trillion of them—to the next Congress? What happens when the buck can't be passed any longer, when Social Security and Medicare beneficiaries start seeing only part of the benefits that they paid their whole working lives to receive in full, and when the pressure that Medicare puts on other parts of the federal budget bursts?

Like hell if any of us know. But I guess the result will answer the question "What happens when you spend half a century electing cowardly leadership to handle your money?"

With every election, the urgency goes up to elect to Congress and the White House real leaders who will govern as though the United States *can't* print money indefinitely. Donald Trump is so far removed from being such a person that it's reasonable to assume he understands the nature of the danger—and willfully ignores it. As the same *Daily Beast* story referenced above noted, one of Trump's campaign advisers for economic issues, Stephen Moore, told the candidate that the United States could confront the debt problem just by helping create a stronger economy: "As Moore recalled, a belief that robust economic growth would solve all problems was the way Trump—starting in 2016—justified the cost of his ambitious proposals to slash taxes, pursue big infrastructure projects, and simply avoid massive cuts to Social Security and Medicare. Since then, the president has continued to show indifference over the national debt, to the consternation of more traditionally conservative associates." [13]

Well, here we are, more than three years later, and the unemployment rate has been at or below 4 percent for several months, the major stock market indices continue to be high— and the federal government is back to running about a $1 trillion budget deficit for the first time since the Obama years and the debt just continues to climb. Growing the economy—which, in turn, grows tax revenue to pay for government spending—is certainly part of the equation for improving the United States' fiscal health. But it can help only so much, relative to what the country already owes and is about to owe to seniors. We know enough about Trump to understand that he won't be moved to change course. "Several people close to the president, both within and outside his administration, confirmed that the national debt has never bothered him in a truly meaningful way, despite his public lip service," the *Daily Beast* piece noted.[14]

His promises on this issue could definitely have been interpreted as mere "lip service" when he signed a two-year spending deal in February 2018 that the Tea Party would've revolted against—and that fiscal conservatives even then protested. The agreement blew through the spending caps previously enshrined in law, hiking federal spending by about $400 billion. The House Freedom Caucus opposed it. "We support funding our troops, but growing the size of government by 13 percent is not what the voters sent us here to do," the group's statement read.[15] So did former senator Jeff Flake, who made his name in the House trying to block largesse. "I will not vote for it. I love bipartisanship, as you know, but the problem is the only time we discover bipartisanship is when we spend more money," he said.[16]

More "lip service" hypocrisy was exposed when Trump did the same thing the following year, approving a government funding act that increased spending by about $320 billion. The Freedom Caucus said no again: "Our country is undeniably headed down a path of fiscal insolvency and rapidly approaching $23 trillion in debt. This is completely unsustainable, and we owe taxpayers and future generations better."[17] Senator

Rand Paul savaged the bill: "Many of the supporters of this debt deal ran around their states for years complaining that President Obama's spending too much and borrowing too much. And these same Republicans now, the whole disingenuous lot of them, will wiggle their way to the front of the draw, to the front of the spending trough to vote for as much or more debt than President Obama ever added."[18]

You know how Trump assessed the situation? By nakedly putting political interest ahead of the good of the country. "Two year deal gets us past the Election. Go for it Republicans, there is always plenty of time to CUT!" he tweeted.[19]

One such time was in May 2018, when the Office of Management and Budget proposed an idea to rescind $15 billion of unused money and "budget authority"—an amount Congress had approved for spending but hadn't actually appropriated yet—from previous years. Mulvaney, then the budget director, talked up the idea in his written notice to the president: "As demonstrated in your first two Budgets, the Administration is committed to ensuring the Federal Government spends precious taxpayer dollars in the most efficient, effective manner possible."[20] (Uh-huh. Sure.) House minority leader Kevin McCarthy called the rescission a step to "restore our fiscal footing." But as Mulvaney himself informed Trump, the net effect of the plan would've been to reduce actual spending by just $3 billion, not $15 billion. In FY 2018, the federal government coughed up $4.1 trillion for its programs. Three billion is 0.07 percent of $4.1 trillion. That's some real "fiscal footing" those guys found.

Nobody can hold Donald Trump uniquely responsible for the United States' sorry budget situation. Its root causes are: allowing federal retirement programs to run on autopilot for decades without allowing for the changes in the country's demographics and economy; expanding the size of government during presidential administrations and Congresses of both parties; a killer financial crisis in 2008 that stomped on tax revenues and put into perspective our fiscal freewheeling as never before; and treating the debt like an afterthought in the budget process, since red ink is rarely a threat in the here and now, voters ultimately don't care about it that much, and, if anything, politicians face the ire of the public for daring to cut things instead of pursuing real reform.

But you'd think that after a rebellion over economic issues in 2010, which brought the Tea Party to DC, having a Republican in the White House would have altered the government's trajectory at least a bit. Not with Trump. Not when that man single-mindedly and stubbornly thinks about budget deficits in entirely the wrong way and when he happily uses the promise of unbroken retirement benefits to help secure the votes of people who may not be around to vote anymore by the time the debt collector comes a-calling. Just don't ever forget this sentence the next time Trump promises not to screw over your children and your children's children with the way he uses taxpayer money: "Yeah, but I won't be here." Those aren't the words of a responsible steward but of a man who has bankrupted companies,[21] is intellectually bankrupt himself, and is nothing more than a self-obsessed charlatan trading the country's future health for his current power. In that respect, Trump referring to himself as "the king of debt" rings true.

Chapter 10

FIXING TRADE

International trade is arguably Donald Trump's pet issue. It's been his fixation for years. "You only have to look at our trade deficit to see that we are being taken to the cleaners by our trading partners," he wrote in his campaign book *The America We Deserve*, published in the year 2000. It was in that election cycle that he contemplated a run for president on the Reform Party ticket. He had the same hubris about the subject then that he does now: "What I would do if elected president would be to appoint myself U.S. trade representative; my lawyers have checked and the president has this authority."* He had the same misunderstanding about trade's mutual benefits: "It's become a cliché to say that business, especially trade, is like war. . . . But cliché or not, it's true." He had the same adversarial tone toward allies: "Germany and Japan were our enemies in World War II, and for decades afterward each was a powerful competitor in trade—tough in peacetime as each had been in war."[1] If you're wondering *Did he really liken fighting Nazis to competing with Germany in the global trade market?* Yes, he really did liken

---

*He in fact has a US trade representative, Robert Lighthizer.

fighting Nazis to competing with Germany in the global trade market.

Misinformed about the nature of basic economics as he's been, though, the way Trump has acted on those beliefs about trade has bolstered the case that he's a strongman whose behavior and personality directly affect the way he governs. Trade is one of the few domestic policies Trump can move just by pushing and pulling levers. On many, if not most, issues, presidents can only set the agenda; they work with leaders of their party in Congress to press a specific cause and then use their enormous political clout to try to get a bill across the finish line. On the rest, they're *supposed* to operate within the constraints that Congress set for them and bureaucracy they oversee. Granted, it seems as though we're always one executive order from federal health care policy swinging one way or the other, having DACA, or using billions of dollars of taxpayer money to build a border wall. But in theory, the president can't create policy from whole cloth unless Congress tells him to.

On trade, presidents do have this kind of power. The Constitution gives the chief executive the ability to negotiate trade deals: "He shall have Power, by and with the Advice and Consent of the Senate, to make Treaties, provided two thirds of the Senators present concur." And although it doesn't grant a similar authority for something like—see if this rings a bell—dealing out tariffs as though they were Halloween candy, Congress, as it has done with so many other of its prerogatives, has passed legislation over the years to allow presidents to take punitive action against trading partners in certain circumstances.

This sure makes it sound as though Trump has a *lot* of room to pursue his trade goals lawfully—and he does, and he has. But what I've aimed to establish in this book—and what a lot of experts on this stuff who are way smarter than me have done in other forums—is that authoritarian behavior is sometimes about pushing the envelope, not breaking it. It's not illegal for the president to say "I alone can fix it"; to say "I have an Article II, where I have to the right to do whatever I want as president"; to say that he has more expertise about a gumbo of unrelated issue areas than anyone else—including generals, if it's the military, lawyers, if it's the court system, or economists, if it's trade. One of the textbook definitions of the word *authoritarian* is "showing a lack of concern for the wishes or opinions of others; domineering; dictatorial." In a system of government in which power is dispersed among three branches and one of those includes 535 elected representatives of the people who are tasked with creating the laws, it's awfully damn suspect that a 536th—the president—would be able to run a one-man show with the advice and counsel of only his "gut" and the lackeys who follow it.

Here's how Trump puts this all into practice—walks the talk, so speak, and not in a good way.

First, there's the "instinct." He wrongly views international trade as a zero-sum game, in which two or more parties aren't all capable of benefiting; instead, someone's gain has to be someone else's loss. "America's relationship with China is at a crossroads. We only have a short window of time to make the tough decisions necessary to keep our standing in the world," he wrote in *Time to Get Tough* (2011). "Roughly every seven years, the Chinese economy doubles in size. That's a tremendous economic achievement, and it's also why they clean our clocks year in and year out on trade."[2] Read that again—the fact that China had grown was *the* reason why the United States had been losing. It's not as though Trump made that argument based on a concern about national security, as one of his top trade advisers, Peter Navarro, has flimsily done, or about a Communist government overtaking the influence of a democratic government in the twenty-first century. The argument instead is about "trade deficits" and another economy "cleaning our clocks" just because it's doing well—the same type of perspective he uses for our relationship with Germany, Japan, or any other US trade partner whose markets have performed, for lack of a more descriptive word, "well." (Remember his exchange with President Moon Jae-in of South Korea: "The United States has trade deficits with many, many countries, and we cannot allow that to continue. And we'll start with South Korea right now. But we cannot allow that to continue. This is really a statement that I make about all trade." *All trade.*)

"The problem is not just that [Trump is] ignorant of the economics (though he is); it's that he appears to sincerely believe the proper way to evaluate whether a policy is working out for the US is to examine not whether it makes the US *better off than it was* but whether it leaves the US *better off relative to other countries*," wrote Vox journalist Dylan Matthews.[3] "The 'great' in 'making America great again' is 'better than the rest,' not 'better,' period."

Second, there's the implementation. A lot of the time, Trump's bluster doesn't make it beyond his Twitter feed or the TV cameras. But with trade, he can put it into practice, working a system in which Congress has provided him and his recent predecessors *tons* of leeway. In January 2018, he imposed tariffs on washing machines and solar panels by using a section of the Trade Act of 1974, which allows him to take action if the International Trade Commission—a federal agency that adjudicates trade disputes and provides expertise to the president and Congress—determines that "increased imports were a substantial cause of serious injury to domestic producers."[4] In March 2018, Trump instituted tariffs on most aluminum and steel imports, citing a provision of the Trade Expansion Act of 1962 that gives him such authority if an executive branch investigation of a specific import finds that it "is being imported into the United States in such quantities or under such circumstances as to threaten to impair the national security."[5] In May 2018, he extended those tariffs to Canada, Mexico, and the European Union, under the same authority.[6] (Canada and Mexico were later exempted.) And throughout 2018 and 2019, he hammered China with several tranches of tariffs on goods that benefit from what the Trade Act of 1974 calls "an act, policy, or practice of a foreign country [that] is unjustifiable and burdens or restricts United States commerce."[7] He used the same reasoning to slap tariffs on $50 billion of Chinese exports in June 2018[8] and $200 billion in September 2018.[9] In May 2019, US trade representative Robert Lighthizer previewed yet another round of action to come: "The President . . . ordered us to begin the process of raising tariffs on *essentially all remaining imports from China*, which are valued at approximately $300 billion." (My emphasis.)[10] Trump made the official announcement in August.

So there you have it: with the power given to him by Congress, the president smacked pretty much the entire world with tariffs on aluminum and steel and hit virtually *everything* coming from China with a tariff. I don't want to get into the merits and demerits of each and every tariff that Trump has levied. Trade is a complicated business, full of domestic and international governing bodies that monitor how world governments subsidize their exports, fool with their currencies, and act in other ways that could give them unfair legs up on the competition. China, no doubt, is a serial offender, and both Republican and Democratic administrations have made their case against the Chinese regime before watchdogs such as the World Trade Organization. All of that is well and good. But the sheer scope of what Trump has done was bound to produce some ill effects for Americans. Consider that, as the administration bragged, the tariffs on washing machines and solar panels were the first to rely on the relevant section of the Trade Act of 1974 in sixteen years; the tariffs on aluminum and steel were essentially worldwide until the government lifted them on Canada and Mexico in May 2019; and the combined tariffs on China, those in effect and those that were promised as of the time of this writing, apply to virtually all Chinese goods the United States imports. As the Congressional Research Service noted, "tariffs fell out of favor in international trade negotiations by the 1970s."[11] That they've come back in the United States with a vengeance is a shock to the world trade market.

How big a shock? *Yuuuge.* According to the nonpartisan think tank the Tax Foundation:

[T]he tariffs imposed so far by the Trump administration would reduce long-run GDP by 0.25 percent ($63.13 billion) and wages by 0.16 percent and eliminate 195,600 full-time equivalent jobs.

If the Trump administration acts on outstanding threats to levy additional tariffs, GDP would fall by an additional 0.34 percent ($84.19 billion), resulting in 0.23 percent lower wages and 261,100 fewer full-time equivalent jobs.

Other countries have announced intentions to impose

tariffs on U.S. exports. If these tariffs are fully imposed, we estimate that U.S. GDP would fall another 0.07 percent ($17.83 billion) and cost an additional 55,300 full-time equivalent jobs.

If all tariffs announced thus far were fully imposed, U.S. GDP would fall by 0.66 percent ($165.15 billion) in the long run, effectively offsetting almost 40 percent of the long-run impact of the Tax Cuts and Jobs Act. Wages would fall by 0.44 percent and employment would fall by 512,000.[12]

Other estimates by Moody's Analytics[13] and Deutsche Bank[14] show similar consequences.

But wait a minute . . . how can this be? You see, tariffs are taxes on American consumers and businesses. Period. They make production more expensive—say, creating something that contains steel and aluminum, so that the higher cost of making the good is passed on in the form of either higher prices or reduced production. How this affects every family and every company naturally varies; some families and companies purchase products warped by tariffs more than others do. But take this sampling of just how unpopular the Trump administration's strategy is among US industries.

Footwear, including NIKE and adidas:

Dear Mr. President:

As leading American footwear companies, brands and retailers, with hundreds of thousands of employees across the U.S., we write to ask that you immediately remove footwear from the most recent Section 301 list published by the United States Trade Representative on May 13, 2019. The proposed additional tariff of 25 percent on footwear would be catastrophic for our consumers, our companies, and the American economy as a whole.

There should be no misunderstanding that U.S. consumers pay for tariffs on products that are imported. As an industry that faces a $3 billion duty bill every year, we can assure you that any increase in the cost of importing shoes has a direct impact on the American footwear consumer. It is an unavoidable fact that as prices go up at the border due to transportation costs, labor rate increases, or additional duties, the consumer pays more for the product.[15]

The outdoor recreation industry:

Representatives from VF Corporation, Columbia Sportswear, Nester Hosiery, and NEMO Equipment met with lawmakers on Capitol Hill this week, letting them know just how hard the U.S.-China trade war is hitting their bottom-line.

"We want our message to get across that this is affecting American businesses, American jobs, American innovation and it's just delaying all of that," said Katie Kumerow, sustainability manager for Nester Hosiery, which manufactures specialty socks.

From September 2018 to July 2019, outdoor recreation businesses have paid $1.8 billion more in tariffs compared to the year ago period, according to new data released Thursday by the Outdoor Industry Association.

This tariff increase is nearly triple what outdoor industry companies paid last year, according to the trade group's latest data.

"Our growth is being hampered right now because we are not able to expand our workforce," says Brent Merriam, Nemo Equipment Chief Operating Officer, who joined fellow association members on Capitol Hill Thursday.[16]

Tech:

The fight with China has had three broad effects, according to Chuck Robbins, the chief executive officer of networking equipment maker Cisco Systems, and the White House has no offsetting positives yet to show for this pain. Surprisingly, perhaps, companies such as Cisco have managed to resist most of the headwinds so far—but that may be changing.

One effect concerns sales to customers in China. US policy was meant to open the market more to American tech companies, but if anything it has had the opposite effect.

Cisco's sales to Chinese telecoms groups had already been sliding for years, but big state-owned enterprises have now shut the door in the company's face. "We're being uninvited to bid, we're not even being allowed to participate any more," Mr. Robbins complained this week.

A second hit has come from the penal tariffs on imports into the US. . . . for suppliers of data centre technology such as Cisco, a recent increase in imports tariffs to 25 per cent has already started to bite.[17]

These examples could continue for a while, especially when it comes to how foreign governments, in particular China, retaliate against the United States. It's been touch and go for our farmers, for instance—things got so bad that the Chinese regime announced in August 2019 that the nation wouldn't buy *any* U.S. agricultural products, to counter Trump's proposal of the latest, $300 billion slate of tariffs on China's exports to the United States. The president of the American Farm Bureau Federation called it "a body blow to thousands of farmers and ranchers"—who, he added, were "already struggling to get by."[18] That's partly reflected by how much US agricultural exports to the mainland have declined in recent years. They peaked at $29.4 billion in FY 2013. They were down to $23.8 billion in FY 2017, which overlapped Trump's first year in office.[19] They declined to $16.3 billion the next fiscal year, when the trade war began; a May 2019 forecast from the Department of Agriculture projected them to be just $6.5 billion in FY 2019.[20] The word *crippling* doesn't even begin to describe the situation.

Although China pledged to reopen its markets to US agriculture throughout the latter part of 2019, pending negotiations with the Trump administration—which included a pledge to lift at least some tariffs on Chinese goods—a load of damage had already been done. Which brings us to . . .

Third, the delusion. You've almost certainly heard the president's quote that "trade wars are good, and easy to win." Here it is in context: "When a country (USA) is losing many billions of dollars on trade with virtually every country it does business with, trade wars are good, and easy to win. Example, when we are down $100 billion with a certain country and they get cute, don't trade anymore—we win big. It's easy!"[21]

Nahhh. It's really not, [commander in] chief. Trump is saying that if the United States happens to be importing a higher value of products from countries than our producers are exporting to them, we *ought* to instigate a trade war with them—which includes the US government doing something like hiking tariffs on them, to which they respond by imposing tariffs or other punitive measures (say, quotas) of their own on US goods, to which we respond, to which they respond. . . . He seems to think that the United States is destined to win such exchanges by default. (After all, he defines "winning big" as "not trading anymore.") How? How will "we win big," much less do it easily, in such a circumstance?

The answer is that we won't. I've already documented some of the numbers that show why. Though they deviate from one another around the margins, the takeaway is unambiguous: we're losers as a result of the trade war Trump has launched on multiple fronts, from Asia to Europe. Because he's a strongman who never owns up to any wrongheaded decision or failure, however, what you hear from him is that *actually*, this playing tit for tat with world economies has been an unqualified success. In other words, what you hear him do is lie.

Take how he's framed the farm bailouts that became necessary specifically because of the trade war. In July 2018, the USDA announced an $11 billion–plus "trade aid" package to farmers to offset the cost of tariffs on China to US agricultural producers. Ten billion dollars of the money was in the form of direct payments, and $1.2 billion went toward buying the surplus products that hadn't been sold to the Chinese.[22] Less than a year later, Secretary of Agriculture Sonny Perdue announced a second round of subsidies, valued at $14.5 billion and $1.4 billion, respectively.[23] There are all sorts of things about this financial assistance to comment on: its merits, its effectiveness, its fairness, how it far exceeds the typical farm subsidies that the government doles out annually. But let's start with how the assistance was framed. Secretary Perdue said, "The plan we are announcing today ensures farmers do not bear the brunt of unfair retaliatory tariffs imposed by China and other trading partners."[24] The words "unfair" and "retaliatory" right next to each other? That's peculiar. Look, I get that the Trump administration's perspective was that China was *already* in the wrong—and it's not incorrect about that, on many levels—and so the United States taxing the Chinese into oblivion was merely "getting even." But what the hell did Team Trump expect to happen in response to a scheme to slap tariffs on almost everything the United States imports from China? Something, to borrow a word, that was "easy" to overcome?

The rhetoric progressed from rationalizing to whitewashing. Just look at how Trump characterized the second round of aid, in May 2019: "Your all time favorite President got tired of waiting for China to help out and start buying from our FARMERS, the greatest anywhere in the World!"[25] But China had already been buying loads of US agricultural products. As recently as 2017, it was the second-largest export market for US food and agriculture.[26] Until the trade war, it bought 60 percent of US soybean exports. It's not as if it hadn't been an active player in the United States' farm industry prior to Trump's election—and it's not as if Trump is due credit for fractionally solving a problem of his own making.

One "tweet storm" in particular, from May 2019, shows how outdated, if not completely bunk, economic thinking has become US policy under Trump. This gonzo theory of economics sounds as though it's from some alternate—or alternatively factual—reality. Let's flag especially troublesome comments with numbers in parentheses and describe them afterward.

Talks with China continue in a very congenial manner—there is absolutely no need to rush—as Tariffs are NOW being paid to the United States by China of 25% on 250 Billion Dollars worth of goods & products. These massive payments go directly to the Treasury of the U.S. . . .

. . . . The process has begun to place additional Tariffs at 25% on the remaining 325 Billion Dollars. The U.S. only sells China approximately 100 Billion Dollars of goods & products, a very big imbalance (1). With the over 100 Billion Dollars in Tariffs that we take in, we will buy. . . . .

. . . . agricultural products from our Great Farmers, in larger amounts than China ever did (2), and ship it to poor & starving countries in the form of humanitarian assistance. In the meantime we will continue to negotiate with China in the hopes that they do not again try to redo deal!

Tariffs will bring in FAR MORE wealth to our Country than even a phenomenal deal of the traditional kind (3). Also, much easier & quicker to do. Our Farmers will do better, faster (4), and starving nations can now be helped (5). Waivers on some products will be granted, or go to new source!

. . . . If we bought 15 Billion Dollars of Agriculture from our Farmers, far more than China buys now, we would have more than 85 Billion Dollars left over for new Infrastructure, Healthcare, or anything else (6).

China would greatly slow down (7), and we would automatically speed up (8)![27]

So that's one, two, three . . . five . . . seven . . . ah, hell. Let's begin in order. This tweet storm:

1. Demonstrates, once more, Trump's misunderstanding of trade deficits. It's one thing to say that another country should open its markets to our businesses; it's another entirely to say that importing more from a country than we export to it is necessarily bad. Let's say this loudly: IT'S NOT. NECESSARILY. BAD.

2. Is an example of Trump bragging about farm welfare. It makes no sense. It's not a competition—at least no competition that a real conservative would ever want to be a part of.

3. Completely ignores the costs of tariffs to the consumers and businesses that were highlighted earlier in this chapter. There's also zero economic evidence that Country 1 bashing Country 2 over the head with tariffs ends up making Country 1 wealthier than do "traditional" trade deals, which I interpret to mean more intelligent ones.

4. Is another statement without evidence.

5. Is just so brazen. In September 2019, it was reported that the Trump administration was about to unveil an overhaul of foreign aid policy to "prioritize countries that 'support' America's goals," wrote *Politico*. "The move would upend at least a generation of largely bipartisan foreign aid policy, *which has long operated under the principle—at least in theory if not always in practice—that financial assistance should prioritize humanitarian need, not political*

allegiance." (My emphasis.)[28] Tired: providing humanitarian aid directly. Wired: providing humanitarian aid by taxing imports at an indirect cost to American consumers and businesses and dedicating a portion of the tariff money to humanitarian aid.*

6. Again ignores that tariffs are essentially taxes on things Americans buy and make. Tariffs are just about the least cost-effective way to raise funds for an initiative such as rebuilding the country's infrastructure.

7. Is the perfect encapsulation of Trump seeing international trade as zero sum. *Somebody else is lagging; we must be gaining!* Not how it works.

8. Is another comment that should make all of us ask "Where is the evidence?" If anything, the evidence shows that the trade war has slowed us down.

I just want to say something really quickly: this is one tweet thread, everybody. One. There are at least eight things in here that make me think "Eh, the President of the United States should be better than that. The president should be smarter than that. The president should at least be more informed than that." This president is not better, not smarter, not more informed—he is lesser, on all counts, for conservatives and for the country.

I wrote a few pages ago that there were many ways to look at Trump's trade aid to the agricultural sector, including its merits and effectiveness and fairness. If you listen to the farm-

---

*Let's not think for a second—not one effing second—that paying for humanitarian aid with tariffs is a "fiscally responsible" way of doing it. Trump did not make that argument, and no one should make it for him. Trump's Republican Party does not give a damn about fiscal conservatism, anyway.

ers on the ground, the assistance has been effective the same way that the government running your grocery store out of the neighborhood and giving you 50 percent of what you would've made otherwise to make up for it is "effective." In July 2019, Trump tweeted, "Farmers are starting to do great again."[29] The president of the Minnesota Corn Growers Association, Brian Thalmann, told Secretary Perdue during a farm forum, "We're not starting to do great again. Things are going downhill and downhill quickly."[30] The *New York Times* reported this in July 2019: "'I think people are generally disappointed to have to get a subsidy,' said Brad Kremer, a soybean farmer from central Wisconsin. 'It's a hardworking, prideful people where I live.' Still, Mr. Kremer said that farmers in Wisconsin were grateful for the assistance because without it, many of them would have gone out of business. Given the difficult economic conditions, he planted only 60 acres of soybeans this year compared with the 600 acres he usually plants."[31]

The fairness of the assistance doesn't seem to grade any higher; an Associated Press review found that large farms found legal workarounds to receive more aid from the first pot of assistance than they were eligible to receive[32] and the initial bailouts were weighted heavily toward soybeans.[33] (In the past, conservatives have called such behavior "picking winners and losers.") The USDA updated its disbursement formula for the second round,[34] and Reuters reported that "widely varying payouts in the second round have confused and irritated farmers nationwide, according to Reuters interviews with more than three dozen growers. Farmers also complained of software problems and poor training of local USDA employees, who have struggled to process applications and payments, farmers and government workers said."[35]

But let's talk a little more about the merits—because they tie into the Trump cult. I've already written why the substance of Trump's trade war is rotten. I haven't elaborated on the origins of it, though, and how they call into question how charitably we should judge the idea of such a thing. One of Trump's top trade advisers, who "has developed a reputation in Washington as a Rasputin-like China hawk who whispers anti-China musings in President Trump's ear," the journalist Alan Rappeport wrote,[36] is the aforementioned Peter Navarro, an economist and the White House's director of trade and manufacturing policy. Navarro is the author of several books, many of which are critical of China and quote anti-Chinese commentary by a person named "Ron Vara." As *The Chronicle of Higher Education* reported in October 2019[37]—and as Navarro himself confirmed[38]—there is no such person as Ron Vara. The name is an anagram of Navarro. Navarro, of course, works for a man who posed as fake spokesmen in phone interactions with reporters.

This, ladies and gentlemen, is supposed to be the United States' dream team for trade.

Navarro, in practice, is the brain behind Trump's adversarial trade policy. Sure, he serves to confirm his boss's suspicions about the issue and so in many ways comes off as merely a yes-man. But Navarro applies the substance to the president's instincts. That substance is tougher, judging by Navarro's words, than even Trump could offer. A story in *Fortune* quotes him: "[E]ven as economic uncertainty has coincided with the tariff tit-for-tat, it seems unlikely that Navarro would suggest that his boss stand down from a trade war. As we hear in [his documentary] 'Death by China,' 'Every time a consumer walks into a Walmart,' says Navarro, 'the first thing they have to do is be aware enough to look for the label. Then when they pick up that good and it says

"Made in China," I want them to think, hmmm, it might either break down or could kill me, number one. [Also], this thing might cost me or someone in my family, or my friend, their job. Lastly, if I buy this, this money is going to go over to help finance what is essentially the most rapid military buildup of a totalitarian regime since when? The thirties.'"[39]

Trump, it should be obvious, is an agitator. Navarro complements him perfectly by being an instigator. Like the president, he has a predetermined set of beliefs about trade and China—many of which are discredited by modern economists—and the eagerness and permission to put them into practice. Anyone that bullheaded about an approach to government policy had better come with at least some sort of acclamation or positive reputation. But as the *Washington Post* reported, he's made enemies with Trump's other economic advisers over his hard-line and unthinking approach to work: "He just makes s—t up," said Trump's former chief economic adviser Gary Cohn, according to former administration officials cited by the *Post*.[40] *Foreign Policy* magazine ran the damning headline "Trump's Top China Expert Isn't a China Expert."[41] And as *The Atlantic* reported, "[E]conomists on both the left and the right say that Navarro's fundamental views of trade are outdated, misguided, or just plain wrong." One of them is former President George W. Bush's economic adviser Greg Mankiw, a professor at Harvard, where an introductory economics course is referred to as "ec 10."

The Atlantic quotes Mankiw as saying "Navarro's understanding of trade economics would not make sense to 'even a freshman at the end of ec 10.'"[42]

"Trust Trump" is bad advice. So is "Trust Navarro." So is "Trust these people on trade."

Chapter 11

FIXING IMMIGRATION

My approach to politics has always been to just say what I think. It's always been about resisting the partisan pressure to toe the party line no matter what, or, in these days of Trump, to support the cult. For example: just on the merits, Donald Trump's harshest skeptics on the left would support a lot of the arguments I've made so far in these pages, such as the ones calling out the president's abuse of power, his white-identity politics, his authoritarian mind-set, and his serial, virtually pathological lying. But that does *not* make them left-wing arguments—or make me anything close to a left-winger. It simply means I belong to a taxonomy that includes a level above my ideological beliefs: my beliefs in the values of democracy. Put it this way: as I've said about the southern border, I want the wall, but if I had to choose between (1) having a wall and having a king or (2) having no wall and having a president, I'd take no wall. I'd take a president over a king. And that is not something I will compromise on.

That's how I want to frame this chapter about immigration. I set out in this book to make a credible argument from the right that *who Trump is* and *what he's done* to our form of government are the most pressing issues facing voters today. Of course, I can't cinch the "credible" part of that unless I convince conservative readers that I, too, am a conservative. I can't think of a better way for someone specifically like me to do it than to talk about the immigration issue, which was a gigantic priority for Trump voters in 2016. It was a gigantic priority for me, too—one of the reasons, in fact, that I voted for him. I believe that the following things about the United States' immigration policy are true:

- It's utterly broken.
- To fix it, one of the solutions we need is a wall along the border with Mexico. As Trump said during a visit to the border in early 2019: "They say 'a wall is medieval.' Well, so is a wheel. . . . There are some things that work. You know what, a wheel works, and a wall works."[1] He's right! You know he's right. You can oppose a wall for a variety of legitimate reasons, but don't say that walls don't work. They do.
- But a wall isn't the be-all, end-all response. We need complementary changes to border enforcement, too, including better technological surveillance and more manpower.
- The backlog in our immigration courts is just outrageous— more than a million cases as of August 2019, the *Wall Street Journal* reported.[2] That's partly the product of a poorly designed process for adjudicating asylum claims, partly the product of putting off deportations, and partly the product of our lacking enough deterrents for illegal immigration in the first place.
- Democrats have failed to address those problems. Republicans have failed to do it. Washington, DC, has failed to do it. Period.

▮ And I agree with President Obama about the nature of becoming and being an American: "We have a right and duty to protect our borders. We can insist to those already here that with citizenship come obligations—to a common language, common loyalties, a common purpose, a common destiny," he wrote in *The Audacity of Hope*.[3]

The bottom line is that I believe in a strong border. I don't believe that anyone should be here illegally. And I believe that people should come here only if they assimilate to the values spelled out in the Declaration of Independence and our Constitution.

But Donald Trump has taken the immigration issue to a dark, bigoted, xenophobic place that no one should welcome. His simplemindedness has reduced the policy portion of it to a single variable (the wall). Since he's incompetent, he hasn't been able to solve for that single variable. He's failed to negotiate for it with Congress. He's violated the Constitution and asked his subordinates to break the law to make up for it. And he's lied about his success with it for all the world to see literally more than two hundred times.[4] But that misrepresentation of reality is ignored by the Trump cult. You can see all his worst traits wrapped up in this: the racial arson, the overestimation of his intellect, the narcissism, the lawbreaking, the alternative facts becoming reality just because he's repeated them enough. This, right here, is the representation of Trump that makes crystal clear that he's not a conservative. He's actually an opportunist. And above all, he's a demagogue.

The debasing way he speaks of immigrants provides one set of evidence. Instead of drawing a line between illegal and legal immigration, he's implied that there's a line between immigrants of color and immigrants from majority-white countries, a line that separates desirable folks from undesirable folks. He's questioned the patriotism of members of Congress specifically because of their immigrant heritage, as when he told a group of congresswomen including representatives Alexandria Ocasio-Cortez, Ilhan Omar, and Rashida Tlaib to "go back and help fix the totally broken and crime infested places from which they came."[5] He's questioned the impartiality of a federal judge overseeing a lawsuit against one of his ventures because Trump wants a wall and the judge is of Mexican descent.[6] He's described entire ethnic groups of nonwhite people as though they have no dignity. Just look at how he generalizes and cheapens the culture of the Middle East: "If Syria wants to fight for their land, that's up to Turkey and Syria, as it has been for hundreds of years, they've been fighting. And the Kurds have been fighting for hundreds of years—that whole mess. It's been going along for a long time. . . . It's a lot of sand. They've got a lot of sand over there. So, there's a lot of sand that they can play with."[7] I don't want to hear the excuse that he was harmlessly imagining a bombed-out haven for terrorists. He could've been describing Jordan or Iraq or Egypt—or Israel. That "lot of sand" is where Jesus came from. That "lot of sand" is where mathematics came from. Trump writes off the worth of people from places abroad that have zero personal value to him. That's an awfully shitty look for the guy who's supposed to be "the leader of the free world."

His demagoguery on immigration extends to government policy, as well. As I said, he's a Johnny-one-note with his opinion of a wall with Mexico. It's the imagery that's attractive to him: "It's going to be a big, fat, beautiful wall," he said who knows how many times during the 2016 presidential campaign.[8] The imagery is attractive to a lot of Americans who are worried about our national identity, too. Sure, you can think that a wall is a practical tool to help stop the flow of immigrants coming here illegally, and I do. But it's a hell of a lot more than that to many people when the idea of a wall sparks a deafening chant of "Build the wall!" at a Trump rally and when Trump says he's going to make Mexico pay for it. That's the demagoguery at work: ripping one prong from a complicated issue of government policy and using it to thump a drum of nativist sentiment. It's an ugly piece of politics.

It's a dumb one, too. Just read the words of John Kelly, who was Trump's secretary of homeland security before becoming White House chief of staff, about how a wall fits into a broader strategy of border security:

- "A physical barrier in and of itself—certainly as a military person that understands defense and defenses—a physical barrier in and of itself will not do the job. It has to be, really, a layered defense. If you were to build a wall from the Pacific to the Gulf of Mexico, you'd still have to back that wall up with patrolling by human beings, by sensors, by observation devices. But as I've said to many of the senators present—and I've said, I think, for three years— really I believe the defense of the southwest border really starts about 1,500 miles south. And that is partnering with some great countries as far south as Peru, really, that are very cooperative with us in terms of getting after the drug production, transport, very, very good with us, to include Mexico."—January 10, 2017, in testimony before the Senate Homeland Security Committee[9]
- "Through the recently released FY 2017 Budget Amendment and the FY 2018 President's Budget currently under development, DHS is seeking to take immediate steps to implement a full complement of solutions to meet border

security requirements. These investments extend beyond physical barriers we think of as wall or fence to include advanced detection capabilities such as surveillance systems, tethered and tactical aerostats, unmanned aircraft systems and ground sensors, all which work in conjunction with improvements to tactical border infrastructure and increased manpower. . . . The barriers work. Technology also works. But all of it doesn't work at all unless you have men and women who are willing to patrol the border, develop relationships, which they do, with their Mexican counterparts directly across the border. . . . It's unlikely that we will build a wall or physical barrier from sea to shining sea, but it is very likely—I'm committed to putting it where the men and women (of DHS) say we should put it."—April 5, 2017, in testimony before the Senate Homeland Security Committee [10]

■ "There's no way, in my view as (Department of Homeland Security) secretary—and I said this in all of my hearings—we don't need a wall from sea to shining sea, as I said. The CBP, Customs and Border Protection people, who are so familiar with the border, they can tell you, you know, if you say, 'I can get you 40 miles,' they'll tell you exactly where they want it. 'I can get you 140 miles,' they can tell you exactly where they want it. If I told them I can get you 2,000 miles, they'd say, 'Eh, seems like an awful waste of money.'"—March 7, 2019, during an event at Duke University [11]

Now, here's the thing about Kelly: He's a retired four-star marine general who was commander, United States Southern Command—the U.S. defense command responsible for operations in Central and South America. The man knows what he's talking about. In fact, that's one of the reasons Trump nominated him to lead DHS: "Trump's team was drawn to him because of his Southwest border expertise," the *Washington Post* reported.[12] There was no questioning his credibility as a tough guy, either; immigration hawks praised his selection,[13] so if *John Kelly* says that simply building a wall can't be an adequate response to our immigration issue . . . then maybe Trump hasn't taken the issue as seriously and as thoughtfully as he should have.

And make no mistake about it—he hasn't. He's never really given a damn about the full range of immigration reform.

If he had, it would have been the first thing he moved on after he was inaugurated. It was, after all, the one subject in the context of "government policy" that defined his run for president and arguably got him elected. More than any other, it was the issue that his base and my radio listeners cared about. And the best he could do was demagogue it by shouting and tweeting "wall, wall, wall" over and over and doing little more, while watching Republicans light themselves on fire in a doomed effort to repeal Obamacare.

If he had *really* ever cared about seeing the wall across the finish line—getting it designed, getting it funded, getting it built—we would've seen some serious progress in the last few years, especially in the first two, when his party controlled both the House and the Senate. There would have been no one for Trump to blame but himself and his fellow Republicans. Instead, any progress has been negligible, particularly if you compare it to the overhaul he promised his voters. What we've gotten in return for casting ballots for him is:

- $341 million in May 2017 "to replace approximately 40 miles of existing primary pedestrian and vehicle border fencing along the southwest border using previously deployed and operationally effective designs, such as currently deployed steel bollard designs, that prioritize agent safety; and to add gates to existing barriers"[14]

- $1.34 billion in March 2018 for "fencing" that uses "operationally effective designs deployed as of [May 2017], such as currently deployed steel bollard designs, that prioritize agent safety"[15]

- $1.38 billion in February 2019 "for the construction of primary pedestrian fencing, including levee pedestrian fencing, in the Rio Grande Valley Sector . . . available for operationally effective designs deployed as of [May 2017], such as currently deployed steel bollard designs, that prioritize agent safety"[16]

That's the extent of Trump's work with Congress: about $3 billion, not for wall but for fence, much of it just to take the place of what was already there, on a project that Customs and Border Protection said they'd need $18 billion to complete[17] and that a bill from House minority leader Kevin McCarthy pegged at $25 billion total.[18]

Quite the negotiator is The Donald.

What makes this choke job even louder is that he reportedly squandered an opportunity to get the full $25 billion in talks with Senate majority leader Chuck Schumer in January 2018.[19] Make what you will of getting the money in exchange for making the Deferred Action for Childhood Arrivals (DACA) program law, as the deal would've done, but Trump blew it so badly that he didn't get a penny after the Democrats' top negotiator approached him. (Senator John Cornyn, the Republicans' number two, said that Schumer had extended the offer; this wasn't some nonexistent thing that the Democrats made up just to make Trump look bad.) All he got was the token funding in the spending legislation referenced above.

So naturally, we come to where this chapter began: I want the wall, but if I had to choose between (1) having a wall and having a king and (2) having no wall and having a president, I'd take no wall. *Trump, who is president, chose to be a king.* After failing to work successfully within the law, he sought to succeed by working outside the law. He declared a bunk "national emergency" on the southern border shortly after he signed the February 2019 spending bill, completely perverting the definition of "emergency" and going around Congress's decision not to give him more funds for the wall than it had already provided. In announcing the emergency, he invoked a statute that allows presidents to move around money that Congress has appropriated for military construction. Some of the projects from which Trump took money include schools for children of active-duty parents, arms ranges, and warehouses for hazardous waste both in the United States and on military bases overseas, as NPR documented.[20] Another is the rebuilding of the Camp Santiago National Guard training base in Puerto Rico, which was pummeled by Hurricane Maria in 2017.[21] Think about this: we've gone from "Mexico is going to pay for the wall" to "Let's take funding from our own military facilities damaged by a natural disaster to pay for the wall."

To Congress's credit, it didn't stand for that. Both the House and the Senate—with the support of twenty-five Republican lawmakers combined—passed a resolution to strike down the emergency declaration. "Never before has a president asked for funding, Congress has not provided it, and the president then has used the National Emergencies Act of 1976 to spend the money anyway," said Republican senator Lamar Alexander of Tennessee, referring to the law that Trump used for the authority to declare his cooked-up emergency.[22] Trump vetoed the resolution, of course, but the declaration continues to be challenged: a Senate committee easily approved legislation in 2019 from Republican senator Mike Lee that would reform the national emergency statutes and end the one that Trump had declared,[23] and a federal judge in Texas ruled against the declaration that October.[24]

You'd think this kind of widespread opposition, which transcends party, would humble the president a bit. You'd *think*. But this is Donald Trump we're talking about. There's not a chance of that. Not only has he broken the law himself in trying to get the wall built, but he's asked others to break it for him. As I mentioned in a previous chapter, he's told his subordinates he'd have their backs if they ran into trouble carrying out unlawful acts on his behalf. "When aides have suggested that some orders are illegal or unworkable, Trump has suggested he would pardon the officials if they would just go ahead, aides said. He has waved off worries about contracting procedures and the use of eminent domain, saying 'take the land,' according to officials who attended the meetings [about the wall]. 'Don't worry, I'll pardon you,' he has told officials in meetings about the wall," the *Washington Post* wrote in August 2019.[25]

That is what he has resorted to, to bring his demagoguery full circle. He's said more than two hundred times that the wall is in the process of being built—even though, as I wrote above, Congress has approved money only for older fence designs that it previously sanctioned. That distinction is important for operational reasons, such as effectiveness, but also because the distinction was *important to Trump*—important enough that he couldn't stop dreaming aloud about how tall and majestic and impenetrable and unprecedented was his vision for a border barrier. In September 2019, Customs and Border Protection told the *Washington Post* that "approximately 64 miles of new border-wall system in place of dilapidated designs" had been erected to date, far short of the 1,000 miles Trump once guaranteed and the 450 miles the administration said would be knocked out by the end of 2020.[26] Yet Trump said as far back as February 2019 that "the chant now should be, 'finish the wall' as opposed to 'build the wall,' because we're building a lot of wall."[27]

Lies, lies everywhere. The story has gone from "The wall must be built and I need $25 billion to do it and I'll get Mexico to pay for it" to "It's being built and when I said Mexico would pay for it I didn't actually mean they'd pay *us* for it and it's paying for it in other ways, anyway." Which is also a lie. Trump said in January 2019 that "Mexico is paying for the Wall through the new USMCA Trade Deal,"[28] even though (1) that trade deal still hadn't been ratified by Congress at the time of this writing, almost a year later, and (2) the deal doesn't include tariffs on Mexican exporters or any levy that would net the United States new money from the Mexican government. (Lies, lies everywhere.) But never mind that, because the story continues. It continues to "The chant should be more like 'finish the wall' at this point, and it's so awesome that 'we're building a wall in Colorado"—he literally said that, "we're building a wall in Colorado"[29] (don't pay attention to this part in parentheses here, but it's not actually a wall). He's selling us a bunch of bullshit, everybody. Don't buy it.

On immigration, Trump has pulled the double whammy of letting down conservatives both on policy outcomes and on the rule of law. For the policy outcomes, he promised a hundred times more than he could deliver, because he failed to think big picture like the vast majority of border hawks *in his own party*—people who said that a wall was a great beginning but certainly not the end of immigration reform. For the rule of law, he resorted to breaching the limits of the presidential office—typical for him—specifically because he failed to follow through on his promises: failed to be even a competent dealmaker with Congress when his party had the majority, much less the greatest dealmaker the world has ever known. So Trump is definitely not worth the trouble. He's a conservative only for show. He has taken legitimate ideas on the right about a complex and sensitive issue such as immigration and demagogued them to hell and back, riffing on them so irresponsibly and prejudicially that he has delegitimized one side of the issue altogether. He provides negative returns on the public's investment in him. And just as I believed it was best to cut my losses with him, I believe it's best that you do, too, if you're wondering about an exit strategy from his camp.

Afterword

CLOSING THOUGHTS

Let's take a trip down memory lane, through the last thirty-plus years of our country's presidential elections. In 1988, the matchup was George H. W. Bush versus Michael Dukakis; in 1992, it was Bush versus Bill Clinton; in 1996, it was Bob Dole versus Clinton; in 2000, it was Bush versus Al Gore; in 2004, it was Bush versus John Kerry; in 2008, it was John McCain versus Barack Obama; in 2012, it was Mitt Romney versus Obama; in 2016, it was Donald Trump versus Hillary Clinton. Up to 2016, there weren't any outliers in that list; you could go back for a while further and still not come across any. Sure, the Bushes and the Clintons were political dynasties, but the politics of each one of them were pretty normal between the center-right and the center-left. Dole, McCain, and Romney were mainstream Republicans, just as Dukakis, Gore, and Kerry were mainstream Democrats, even if it was up for debate *just how* conservative or *just how* liberal each one was. Obama provoked a political rebuke stronger than any of his recent predecessors had, of which I was a part. There might not be a major US political figure in my lifetime with whom I've disagreed more strongly than him. But he had a coherent, sane worldview, and I consider him a patriotic American.

Trump is the one person from this list who stands way, way apart from the rest. But it's not because he was a businessman who had never held elected office—the kind of "outsider" that antiestablishment voters have long pined for to "shake up the system." It's because at no point in Trump's *life* did he ever develop a basic understanding and appreciation for our form of government—for democracy. He has never been one to play by the rules. And when he took that instinct into a job requiring that he uphold the Constitution and the laws of the United States, which he neither understands nor cares about, our country almost seemed destined to take a tumultuous ride for the following few years. I didn't foresee the scope of that possibility in 2016—but I sure as hell see it in the rearview mirror now.

His rise means one thing: for the first time in memory, Americans are not choosing between just a Republican and a Democrat. Both parties can scream about the threat the other poses to the country, but their warnings apply to government policy. Republicans worry about Democrats nationalizing medical insurance, just as Democrats worry about Republicans repealing Obamacare. They can each say that their opponents' ideas are mortal threats to the United States—and as someone who comes from the world of talk radio, I grant that this kind of overstatement often doesn't do the public's mood any favors. But ultimately, this kind of disagreement is over legislation that Congress should pass. I side with the Republican point of view on most such issues. *But those are not the issues that define Donald Trump.*

Trump is defined not by his stance on health care reform but by his flagrant abuse of his office's powers. He is defined not by his trade strategy but by his narcissism, which liberates him to behave however he damn well pleases. He is defined not by the Tax Cuts and Jobs Act but by his cult of personality, which resembles that of historical and contemporary authoritarians and even dictators. He is not part of the kind of binary choice that Americans are used to making between the two major parties. He is part of something much, much broader and history bending: a choice between a president and a wannabe tyrant, between democracy and despotism.

Look—I straight-up disagree with the Democratic Party about *a lot* of things. I'm troubled that its left flank, which makes economic promises that the government could never keep, is gaining so much influence in its ranks. I'm downright disturbed that two-thirds of American adults can't accurately define socialism, per a YouGov survey from October 2019, and that 70 percent of millennials say they would vote for self-described socialists.[1] This tells me that too much of the country doesn't adequately appreciate the damage that socialism has done to people worldwide and so is okay with some idea of it at home. Even if that idea is unlikely to ever manifest as anything close to the real thing, a strong turn toward progressive government is enough for me to say, "Hell, no."

But in these times, I have to ask myself: *Where does the importance of this rank in comparison to the survival of our government?* I've already stated that I'd rather have no border wall with Mexico if the trade-off is having a king instead of a president. What if the point of view were flipped, though? I can live with Washington failing to enact conservative policy, as frustrating as that outcome is. But what about Washington veering left? After all, avoiding that is one side of the bargain many Republicans felt they had to make in 2016: accept Trump if only to reject Hillary Clinton's vision for the United States.

There are a few things I want to emphasize. One: Weighing almost the entirety of government policy against the health of that very government is an apples-to-apple-tree comparison. If the tree rots and dies, there are no apples left to pick—no wall to build, no trade deals to ratify, no taxes to cut. This applies even to the more existential problems facing the country, such as long-term federal debt reduction and climate change. Of course we need to address those at the same time as we work on repairing our nation's democracy. *But unless we have a stable, democratic form of government,* we won't be able to tackle those matters in the long run. Now, maybe some voters' preference is that a president try to take care of these big things alone, since Congress stubbornly can't or won't act in a way that aligns with their viewpoint. Supporting Trump's emergency declaration for the southern border is an example of such a preference in action. So is supporting Tom Steyer's pledge to reform the nation's climate agenda with executive orders. In these cases, Trump's backers and Steyer's backers may applaud their actions. That's how it goes with a king sometimes: sometimes he'll give you what you want, and you'll cheer.

But when he doesn't, you'll jeer—and you won't have any recourse.

And when he behaves unbound by the rule of law altogether and unaccountable to the citizenry, you'll be living not in a democracy but in the type of society the Founding Fathers fled so they and their successors would never have to endure anything like it again.

The second thing I want to emphasize is that Donald Trump is not a banner man for conservatism. It's my opinion that conservatives' strongest objection to him should be that he acts like a dictator. Go through the history of the presidency, and recall all the legitimate objections that we had to Trump's predecessors behaving in such a fashion. Conservatives *despise* the legacy of Woodrow Wilson, and rightly so. We hold in contempt Franklin D. Roosevelt's Supreme Court–packing scheme and unlawful internment of immigrants and nationals of Japanese, German, and Italian ancestry during World War II—something he authorized with an executive order. "WHEREAS the successful prosecution of the war requires every possible protection against espionage and against sabotage to national-defense material, national-defense premises, and national-defense utilities," it began.[2] You can trace this kind of paranoia all the way back to the Alien and Sedition Acts, which, although approved by Congress, carried with them a nativist sentiment away from which the United States has tried to evolve over the decades. It's because of *this exact history* that conservatives' antennae should be up during the time of Trump. We've been down these treacherous roads before. We shouldn't have to travel down them ever again. If our value system *truly* places the Constitution and the law at the fore and is summed up by the aspirational words of our Founders that we claim to hold so dear, we have to reject Donald Trump wholesale. It's not summed up just by that one sentence of the Declaration of Independence that we're so familiar with: "We hold these truths to be self-evident, that all men are created equal, that they are endowed by their Creator with certain unalienable Rights, that among these are Life, Liberty and the pursuit of Happiness." It's the one that comes right after: "That to secure these rights, Governments are instituted among Men, deriving their just powers from the consent of the governed." Trump exercises his powers unjustly and acts without Congress's consent where it's required—the Congress, made up of representatives the people choose to make laws on their behalf.

Not only does enabling Donald Trump go against what we believe as conservatives about the rule of law and not of men; it's counterproductive to our future priorities. For four years, he has thoroughly destroyed the reputation of conservatism—not because he embodies it but because he bastardizes it. And the Republicans in Washington who should defend conservative values instead of him consistently choose wrong. One prominent example that comes to mind is Republican senator Thom Tillis of North Carolina, who published an excellent critique of Trump's emergency declaration on the southern border—defending the idea of a wall with Mexico but not the unconstitutional way the president wanted to build it. This essentially was my position to a T. "It is my responsibility to be a steward of the Article I branch, to preserve the separation of powers and to curb the kind of executive overreach that Congress has allowed to fester for the better part of the past century," he wrote. "I stood by that principle during the Obama administration, and I stand by it now."[3]

Bingo!

"Conservatives rightfully cried foul when President Barack Obama used executive action to completely bypass Congress and unilaterally provide deferred action to undocumented adults who had knowingly violated the nation's immigration laws. Some prominent Republicans went so far as to proclaim that Obama was acting more like an 'emperor' or 'king' than a president," he continued. "There is no intellectual honesty in now turning around and arguing that there's an imaginary asterisk attached to executive overreach—that it's acceptable for my party but not thy party."[4]

Bingo! Bingo, bingo, bingo!

But Tillis faced a political cost for having the chutzpah to be, I dunno, a *consistent conservative.* "Conservative" activists in North Carolina murmured about supporting a primary challenger to the incumbent. It appeared for a while that a staunch Trump ally, Representative Mark Walker, would be the guy: "North Carolina Republican primary voters have made their voices clear. They stand with the President. Our senators should, as well," he told *The Hill.*[5] Tillis should've held his head high for doing the right thing—and not backed down. Because if so many people in politics would like to delude themselves into thinking that they'd stand up for "country over party," we need examples of people walking the talk. Yet Tillis didn't. He yielded and, three weeks after his op-ed was printed, voted to support the president's declaration.[6] Walker declined to go up against Tillis,[7] and Trump tweeted his endorsement of the incumbent a couple of weeks later.[8]

These "thirty pieces of silver" examples are rampant among Republicans these days. My urging to conservatives: Let's be better than that. If a Democratic president tries to significantly alter the country just through executive action, too many of us won't have the credibility to call it out. If Trump continues to demagogue the immigration issue and we go along with him, we will consign the Republican Party to being an ass-backwards group of xenophobes *for a generation.* If we keep letting the government under his leadership run budget deficits as high as a trillion dollars even in economically good times, we won't have a lick of standing to cry foul about the exploding debt in the long term. *If we keep letting all this happen* . . . we're letting conservatism die so we can have Donald Trump.

There's no chance in hell that I would make that trade.

This brings me to the third thing I want to emphasize: our country can withstand four years of a president named "Trump";

giving him another term may do it irreparable damage. It isn't the case that conservatism will live only as long as Trump continues to be president. Around the country, in state houses and governorships, and in the US Congress, I want to see conservative ideas flourish. I want to see patriotic, conservative officials stand up to liberal excesses where they threaten to undermine "the general welfare" mentioned in our Constitution, which could happen under a Democratic president. It's for these reasons that when I say I'd rather have a president than a king no matter what, I'd rather have even a *socialist* president than a king—than a person whose worst-case scenario is to plunge our nation deeper toward one-man rule. It becomes more difficult over time for the counterbalances and sources of accountability in our political system—namely, Congress, the courts, and the voters—to constrain such a person. *But they'll always be able to constrain that person as long as he behaves like a president, even if his agenda is bad.* When it comes to making policy, there are all sorts of gears grinding against each other that keep radical ideas in check. It's how the system works; it's why, most years, this country has been a pretty stable place.

Being the people who make laws and being the person who enforces those laws are two completely different gigs. The second job has an enormous amount of power that the Founding Fathers expected would be used responsibly. If that power is misused instead—to enrich or corruptly protect the person holding the office, to get back at political opponents, to play Congress's role rather than letting Congress do it—our country teeters on disaster every minute. I can't predict exactly what the years 2021 to 2025 will look like if Trump is president for all of them. I *can* say that all of the madness we've experienced for the last three-plus years will become more severe. If our political system does not hold him accountable for serially abusing it, he will go on abusing it—worse and worse, since there will be nothing to stop him but partisan opposition, however effective it might be.

Saying no to Donald Trump should not be a partisan project. That's because Americans can never condone a dictator. By the time this book comes out, there is a strong chance that he will have been impeached by the House of Representatives, and the political rhetoric of him, his supporters, and his adversaries will have grown more heated. We all need to remove ourselves from that zoo of minute-by-minute, back-and-forth shouting. We need to gain perspective and see Trump for what he fully is: a wannabe tyrant who will abuse his authority to get what he wants; a narcissist who is incapable of or resistant to making informed decisions that affect the course of the United States; the center of a dangerous cult that espouses and is supported by complete lies, as if fabrication is his first language; a bully and a bigot; a man who is unqualified to be the steward of this nation that the presidency requires; a man who is untrustworthy and unfit to be our commander in chief. Deciding whether or not to empower him is deciding whether or not to support our democracy. This particular binary choice could not be clearer.

If you're in Trump's corner but are wondering about the wisdom of remaining there—or if you have been undecided about these last few complicated years of politics but sense that there is something uniquely wrong about Trump—then please let me offer two blunt words of encouragement: Fuck silence.

It's time to speak up. This president is exactly the type of ruler that our Founders feared. It's therefore on all of us to put our nation's interest before party, policy outcomes, political satisfaction, disgust with our culture—before a man who says he looks out for you while in reality he looks out only for himself.

Fuck silence. Country first.

Acknowledgments

This book is about speaking up. About the imperative of speaking up. About having the courage to speak up. About speaking up even when you know that it will hurt you financially, professionally, and politically to do so. It's about placing country first.

To this end, this book would not have been written without the courage of those who came before me who refused to remain silent and who spoke up against party—against their political interests. They should be acknowledged. I think of Margaret Chase Smith, the newly elected Republican senator from Maine who, in 1950, stood and denounced a demagogic senator from her own party named McCarthy. I think of that group of Republican members of Congress, including Barry Goldwater, who in 1974 had the courage to pay a visit to the White House, a visit that made clear to a president from their own party that he had better resign or face impeachment.

I think of the courage of all those "Never Trumpers," who, from the very beginning—from the moment he rode down that escalator in the summer of 2015—spoke publicly against then-candidate Donald Trump. I think of elected officials like Senator Jeff Flake, and political commentators like Bill Kristol, who understood from the beginning the threat this person was to our Republic. Contrary to what the Trump grifters will tell you, it does not benefit a Republican's or a conservative's career to publicly oppose Trump. All those who sacrificed their livelihoods by refusing to remain silent against Trump deserve a huge thanks.

Finally, I think of all those of those—including myself—who have had the courage over the course of these past three years to publicly admit our mistake in supporting Trump and pledge to oppose him, on the record and out loud. Better late than never to have the courage to speak up.

Notes

INTRODUCTION: OPENING MONOLOGUE

1. "How Journalists See Journalists in 2004: Views on Profits, Performance and Politics," Pew Research Center for the People & the Press, May 2004, https://www.pewresearch.org/wp-content/uploads/sites/4 /legacy-pdf/214.pdf; Lars Willnat and David H. Weaver, "The American Journalist in the Digital Age: Key Findings," Indiana University School of Journalism, 2014, http://archive.news.indiana.edu/releases /iu/2014/05/2013-american-journalist-key-findings.pdf.

2. Donald J. Trump (@realDonaldTrump), tweet, September 1, 2019, https://twitter.com/realDonaldTrump/status/1168174613827899393.

3. Donald Trump, "Remarks by President Trump in Briefing on Hurricane Dorian," White House, September 1, 2019, https://www.white house.gov/briefings-statements/remarks-president-trump-briefing -hurricane-dorian/.

4. "DORIAN Graphics Archive: 5-day Forecast Track, Initial Wind Field and Watch/Warning Graphic," National Hurricane Center and Central Pacific Hurricane Center, https://www.nhc.noaa.gov/archive /2019/DORIAN_graphics.php?product=5day_cone_with_line_and _wind.

5. Donald J. Trump (@realDonaldTrump), tweet, September 4, 2019, https://twitter.com/realDonaldTrump/status/1169375550806351872.

6. Donald J. Trump (@realDonaldTrump), tweet, September 5, 2019, https://twitter.com/realDonaldTrump/status/1169705282123046913.

7. Donald J. Trump (@realDonaldTrump), video, September 6, 2019, https://twitter.com/realDonaldTrump/status/1170089069105340416.

8. Andrew Freedman and Jason Samenow, "An Absence of Meteorologists at Trump's Hurricane Dorian Briefings May Have Helped Lead to the Alabama Tweet Fiasco," *Washington Post*, September 17, 2019, https://www.washingtonpost.com/weather/2019/09/17/an-absence-meteorologists-trumps-hurricane-dorian-briefings-may-have-helped-lead-alabama-tweet-fiasco/.

9. "Statement from NOAA," National Oceanic and Atmospheric Administration, September 6, 2019, https://www.noaa.gov/news/statement-from-noaa.

10. Peter Baker, Lisa Friedman, and Christopher Flavelle, "Trump Pressed Top Aide to Have Weather Service 'Clarify' Forecast That Contradicted Trump," *New York Times*, September 11, 2019, https://www.nytimes.com/2019/09/11/us/politics/trump-alabama-noaa.html.

11. Jim Swift (@JimSwiftDC), "Salena Zito is beyond fucking parody," tweet, September 6, 2019, https://twitter.com/JimSwiftDC/status/1170178035196338177.

12. Kevin Schaul and Kevin Urhmacher, "The Complete List of GOP Lawmakers Reacting to Trump's 'Go Back' Tweet," *Washington Post*, July 20, 2019, https://www.washingtonpost.com/graphics/2019/politics/trump-go-back-gop-reactions-list/.

CHAPTER 1: THE LIES

1. Sean Spicer, "Statement by Press Secretary Sean Spicer," White House, January 21, 2017, https://www.whitehouse.gov/briefings-statements/statement-press-secretary-sean-spicer/.

2. "Full Text: Trump, Pence Remarks at CIA Headquarters," *Politico*, January 2, 2017. https://www.politico.com/story/2017/01/full-text-trump-pence-remarks-cia-headquarters-233978

3. Tim Wallace, Karen Yourish, and Troy Griggs, "Trump's Inauguration vs. Obama's: Comparing the Crowds," *New York Times*, Janu-

ary 20, 2017, https://www.nytimes.com/interactive/2017/01/20/us/politics/trump-inauguration-crowd.html.

4. Spicer, "Statement by Press Secretary Sean Spicer."

5. Ibid.

6. Lisa Desjardins (@LisaDNews), tweet, January 20, 2017, https://twitter.com/LisaDNews/status/822485418482483201; Gillian Brockell (@gbrockell), tweet, January 20, 2017, https://twitter.com/gbrockell/status/822474693361987584.

7. Metro (@wmata), tweet, January 20, 2017, https://twitter.com/wmata/status/822482330346487810.

8. "Meet the Press 01/22/17," NBC News, January 22, 2017, https://www.nbcnews.com/meet-the-press/meet-press-01-22-17-n710491.

9. Spicer, "Statement by Press Secretary Sean Spicer."

10. Ibid.

11. http://www.trumptwitterarchive.com/archive/fake%20news%20%7C%7C%20fakenews%20%7C%7C%20fake%20media/ttff/1-19-2017.

12. Donald J. Trump (@realDonaldTrump), tweet, November 27, 2016, https://twitter.com/realDonaldTrump/status/802972944532209664.

13. Cristina Tardáguila, "Trump's 9/11 Memories Aren't Fact-Based—and Fact-Checkers Wrote About Them Again This Year," Poynter, September 13, 2019, https://www.poynter.org/fact-checking/2019/trumps-9-11-memories-arent-fact-based-and-fact-checkers-wrote-about-them-again-this-year/.

14. Jon Greenberg, "Donald Trump's Ridiculous Link Between Cancer, Wind Turbines," PolitiFact, April 8, 2019, https://www.politifact.com/truth-o-meter/statements/2019/apr/08/donald-trump/republicans-dismiss-trumps-windmill-and-cancer-cla/.

15. Glenn Kessler and Joe Fox, "The False Claims that Trump Keeps Repeating," *Washington Post*, October 9, 2019. https://www.washingtonpost.com/graphics/politics/fact-checker-most-repeated-disinformation/.

16. Donald J. Trump, "Remarks by President Trump in Joint Address to Congress," White House, February 28, 2017, https://www.whitehouse.gov/briefings-statements/remarks-president-trump-joint-address-congress/.

17. Executive Order 13780: *Protecting the Nation from Foreign Terrorist Entry into the United States*: Initial Section 11 Report, US Department of Justice, January 2018, https://www.justice.gov/opa/press-release/file/1026436/download.

18. Donald J. Trump (@realDonaldTrump), tweet, January 16, 2018, https://twitter.com/realDonaldTrump/status/953406553083777029.

19. https://www.documentcloud.org/documents/5674047-DOJ-Response-Re-Reconsideration-122118.html.

20. Donald J. Trump (@realDonaldTrump), tweet, September 15, 2019, https://twitter.com/realDonaldTrump/status/1173371482812162048.

21. Jake Tapper (@jaketapper), ".VP Pence to me on @CNNSotu in June," Tweet, September 16, 2019. https://twitter.com/jaketapper/status/1173628093052964871?lang=en.

22. "America's Newsroom with Bill Hemmer and Sandra Smith," Archive, August 28, 2019. https://archive.org/details/FOXNEWSW_20190828_130000_Americas_Newsroom_With_Bill_Hemmer_and_Sandra_Smith/start/6120/end/6180.

23. James s. Brady Press Briefing Room, "Press Briefing by Secretary of State Mike Pompeo and Secretary of the Treasury Steven Mnuchin," White House Press Briefings, September 10, 2019. https://www.whitehouse.gov/briefings-statements/press-briefing-secretary-state-mike-pompeo-secretary-treasury-steven-mnuchin/.

24. Ibid.

25. "Remarks by President Trump and Prime Minister Conte of Italy in Joint Press Conference," White House Remarks, July 30, 2018. https://www.whitehouse.gov/briefings-statements/remarks-president-trump-prime-minister-conte-italy-joint-press-conference/, Meet the Press (@MeetThePress), "WATCH: Trump tells Chuck Todd that he wants to talk with Iran," Tweet, June 23, 2019. https://twitter.com/MeetThePress/status/1142820376734523393.

CHAPTER 2: THE CONSTITUTION BREAKER

1. Joel Beall, "10 Astonishing Claims from the Book Detailing President Trump's Cheating at Golf," *Golf Digest*, April 4, 2019, https://www.golfdigest.com/story/10-astonishing-claims-from-the-book-detailing-president-trumps-cheating-at-golf.

2. Donald J. Trump, "Remarks by President Trump at Turning Point USA's Teen Student Action Summit 2019," White House, July 23, 2019, https://www.whitehouse.gov/briefings-statements/remarks-president-trump-turning-point-usas-teen-student-action-summit-2019/.

3. "Trump's 2,000 Conflicts of Interest (and Counting)," Citizens for Responsibility and Ethics in Washington, https://www.citizensforethics.org/2000-trump-conflicts-of-interest-counting/.

4. Megan Cassidy, "Arpaio Found Guilty of Criminal Contempt," *The Republic*, July 31, 2017, https://www.azcentral.com/story/news/local/phoenix/2017/07/31/maricopa-county-sheriff-joe-arpaio-found-guilty-criminal-contempt-court/486278001/.

5. "Pardons Granted by President Trump," United States Department of Justice, https://www.justice.gov/pardon/pardons-granted-president-donald-trump.

6. John Dickerson, "A Phony Murder Plot Against Joe Arpaio Winds Up Costing Taxpayers $1.1 Million," *Phoenix New Times*, October 28, 2008, https://www.phoenixnewtimes.com/news/a-phony-murder-plot-against-joe-arpaio-winds-up-costing-taxpayers-11-million-6629798.

7. Shaun Attwood, "Sheriff Joe Arpaio Brags His Tent City Jail Is a Concentration Camp," YouTube, December 7, 2010, https://www.youtube.com/watch?v=D7reZOp2Qco.

8. Robert S. Mueller, "Report on the Investigation into Russian Interference in the 2016 Presidential Election," vol. 1, US Department of Justice, March 2019, https://www.justice.gov/storage/report.pdf, 131.

9. Ibid., 134.

10. Maggie Haberman, Annie Karni, and Eric Schmitt, "Trump Urged

Homeland Security Official to Close Border Despite an Earlier Promise of a Delay," *New York Times*, April 12, 2019, https://www.nytimes.com/2019/04/12/us/politics/trump-border.html.

11. Nick Miroff and Josh Dawsey, "'Take the Land': President Trump Wants a Border Wall. He Wants It Black. And He Wants It by Election Day," *Washington Post*, August 27, 2019, https://www.washingtonpost.com/immigration/take-the-land-president-trump-wants-a-border-wall-he-wants-it-black-and-he-wants-it-by-election-day/2019/08/27/37b80018-c821-11e9-a4f3-c081a126de70_story.html.

12. "Excerpts from the Times's Interview with Trump," *New York Times*, July 19, 2017, https://www.nytimes.com/2017/07/19/us/politics/trump-interview-transcript.html.

13. Donald J. Trump (@realDonaldTrump), tweet, July 25, 2017, https://twitter.com/realDonaldTrump/status/889790429398528000.

14. Donald J. Trump (@realDonaldTrump), tweet, July 26, 2017, https://twitter.com/realDonaldTrump/status/890207082926022656; tweet, July 26, 2017, https://twitter.com/realDonaldTrump/status/890208319566229504.

15. Jordain Carney, "GOP Senator: Cuccinelli Couldn't Win Senate Confirmation," *The Hill*, June 10, 2019, https://thehill.com/homenews/senate/447779-gop-senator-cuccinelli-couldnt-win-senate-confirmation.

16. "Transcript: President Trump on 'Face the Nation,'" February 3, 2019, CBS News, https://www.cbsnews.com/news/transcript-president-trump-on-face-the-nation-february-3-2019/.

17. Tim Alberta, *American Carnage: On the Front Lines of the Republican Civil War and the Rise of President Trump* (New York: Harper, 2019), 347.

18. "Presidential Proclamation on Declaring a National Emergency Concerning the Southern Border of the United States," White House, February 15, 2019, https://www.whitehouse.gov/presidential-actions/presidential-proclamation-declaring-national-emergency-concerning-southern-border-united-states/.

19. Miroff and Dawsey, "'Take the Land.'"

CHAPTER 3: THE CONSTITUTION BREAKER, PART TWO

1. "Freedom of Expression," ACLU. https://www.aclu.org/other/free dom-expression.

2. "Fake News," Trump Twitter Archive, http://www.trumptwitter archive.com/archive/fake%20news/ftff/1-20-2017_9-21-2019. "enemy of the people," Trump Twitter Archive, http://www.trumptwitterar chive.com/archive/enemy%20of%20the%20people/ftff/1-20-2017_9 -21-2019. Michael M. Grynbaum, "Trump Renews Pledge to 'Take a Strong Look' at Libel Laws," *New York Times*, January 10, 2018, https://www.nytimes.com/2018/01/10/business/media/trump-libel -laws.html. Margaret Harding McGill and Daniel Lippman, "White House Drafting Executive Order to Tackle Silicon Valley's Alleged Anti-conservative Bias," *Politico*, August 7, 2019, https://www.po litico.com/story/2019/08/07/white-house-tech-censorship-1639051. Corinne Ramey, "President Trump Can't Block Twitter Users, Federal Appeals Court Rules," *Wall Street Journal*, July 9, 2019, https://www .wsj.com/articles/president-trump-cant-block-twitter-users-federal -appeals-court-rules-11562685206. Mathew Ingram, "White House Revokes Press Passes for Dozens of Journalists," *Columbia Journalism Review*, May 9, 2019, https://www.cjr.org/the_media_today/white -house-press-passes.php. Mike Calia, "Trump Calls for a Boycott of AT&T to Force 'Big Changes' at CNN," CNBC, June 3, 2019, https://www.cnbc.com/2019/06/03/trump-calls-for-a-boycott-of-att -to-force-big-changes-at-cnn.html.

3. Jon Allsop, "A Circus, and What Matters," *Columbia Journalism Review*, July 12, 2019, https://www.cjr.org/the_media_today/trump-so cial-media-summit.php.

4. Donald J. Trump, "Remarks by President Trump at the Presidential Social Media Summit," White House, July 11, 2019, https://www .whitehouse.gov/briefings-statements/remarks-president-trump-pres idential-social-media-summit/.

5. Howard Kurtz, Michael Dobbs, and James V. Grimaldi, "In Rush to

Air, CBS Quashed Memo Worries," *Washington Post*, September 19, 2004, http://www.washingtonpost.com/wp-dyn/articles/A31727 -2004Sep18.html.

6. Howard Witt, "True or False: Blogs Always Tell It Straight," *Chicago Tribune*, September 19, 2004, https://www.chicagotribune.com/news /ct-xpm-2004-09-19-0409190265-story.html.

7. "United States District Court, Southern District of New York," *PEN AMERICAN CENTER, INC., v. Donald J. Trump*, February 6, 2019, https://pen.org/wp-content/uploads/2019/02/PEN-America-v -Trump-Amended-Complaint-2.6.19.pdf, 6.

8. Michael M. Grynbaum and Elizabeth Williamson, "Trump Adminis-tration Uses Misleading Video to Justify Barring of CNN's Jim Acosta," *New York Times*, November 8, 2018, https://www.nytimes.com/2018/11 /08/business/media/infowars-white-house-jim-acosta-cnn.html.

9. Dana Milbank, "The White House Revoked My Press Pass. It's Not Just Me—It's Curtailing Access for All Journalists," *Washington Post*, May 8, 2019, https://www.washingtonpost.com/opinions/the-white -house-has-revoked-my-press-pass-its-not-just-me—its-curtailing -access-for-all-journalists/2019/05/08/bb9794b4-71c0-11e9-8be0 -ca575670e91c_story.html.

10. David Jackson, "Donald Trump Says He May Revoke Press Creden-tials for Other Reporters, Not Just CNN's Jim Acosta," *USA Today*, November 9, 2018, https://www.usatoday.com/story/news/politics /2018/11/09/donald-trump-threatens-other-reporters-white-house -press-passes/1942013002/.

11. Milbank, "The White House Revoked My Press Pass. It's Not Just Me—It's Curtailing Access for All Journalists."

12. Byron Tau, "Judge Grants CNN's Motion to Restore Jim Acosta's White House Press Pass," *Wall Street Journal*, November 16, 2018, https://www.wsj.com/articles/judge-grants-cnns-motion-to-restore -jim-acostas-white-house-press-pass-1542381937.

13. "Gorka to Karem: 'You're Not a Journalist, You're a Punk,'" *Wash-ington Post*, July 11, 2019, https://www.youtube.com/watch?v=zRog WTuS5HI.

14. Josh Gerstein, "Judge Tells White House to Reinstate Reporter's Pass," *Politico*, September 3, 2019, https://www.politico.com/story/2019/09/03/judge-press-pass-brian-karem-1479990.

15. Donald J. Trump (@realDonaldTrump), tweet, January 24, 2017, https://twitter.com/realdonaldtrump/status/824078417213747200.

16. Donald J. Trump (@realDonaldTrump), tweet, July 1, 2017, https://twitter.com/realdonaldtrump/status/881273362454118400.

17. Donald J. Trump (@realDonaldTrump), tweet, December 9, 2017, https://twitter.com/realdonaldtrump/status/939485131693322240.

18. Donald J. Trump (@realDonaldTrump), tweet, June 2, 2018, https://twitter.com/realdonaldtrump/status/1002954515941941249.

19. Amy B. Wang, "Trump Retweets Image Depicting 'CNN Squashed Beneath His Shoe,'" *Washington Post*, December 24, 2017, https://www.washingtonpost.com/news/the-fix/wp/2017/12/24/trump-retweets-image-depicting-cnn-squashed-beneath-his-shoe/.

20. "Trump Retweets, Deletes Questionable Posts," CNN, August 15, 2017, https://www.cnn.com/videos/politics/2017/08/15/donald-trump-twitter-train-cnn-logo-delete.cnn.

21. Donald J. Trump (@realDonaldTrump), tweet, July 2, 2017, https://twitter.com/realDonaldTrump/status/881503147168071680.

22. Jon Allsop, "A Deadly Year for Mexico's Journalists," *Columbia Journalism Review*, August 27, 2019, https://www.cjr.org/the_media_today/mexico_journalist_murders.php; Carolina de Assis, "Brazilian Journalists Receive Death Threats After Publishing Reports Critical of the Armed Forces," Journalism in the Americas, April 11, 2019, https://knightcenter.utexas.edu/blog/00-20719-brazilian-journalists-receive-death-threats-after-publishing-reports-critical-armed-fo.

23. Donald J. Trump (@realDonaldTrump), tweet, June 3, 2019, https://twitter.com/realdonaldtrump/status/1135499002626154496.

24. Sean Spicer, "Statement by Press Secretary Sean Spicer," White House, January 21, 2017, https://www.whitehouse.gov/briefings-statements/statement-press-secretary-sean-spicer/.

25. Brian Stelter, "Donald Trump Rips into Possible Warner Deal," CNN,

October 22, 2016, https://money.cnn.com/2016/10/22/media/donald -trump-att-time-warner/.

26. Brent Kendall and Drew FitzGerald, "Justice Department Files Lawsuit Challenging AT&T–Time Warner Deal," *Wall Street Journal*, November 20, 2017, https://www.wsj.com/articles/justice-department-expected-to -file-lawsuit-challenging-at-t-time-warner-deal-1511210955.

27. Jane Mayer, "The Making of the Fox News White House," *The New Yorker*, March 11, 2019, https://www.newyorker.com/magazine/2019 /03/11/the-making-of-the-fox-news-white-house.

28. Ibid.

29. David Shepardson, "White House Will Not Turn Over Documents on AT&T–Time Warner Merger," Reuters, April 16, 2019, https://www.reuters.com/article/us-time-warner-at-t-congress/white -house-will-not-turn-over-documents-on-att-time-warner-merger -idUSKCN1RS28R.

30. Jan Wolfe, "Trump Threatens to Sue CNN, Seeks 'Substantial' Payment over Damages: Letter," Reuters, October 18, 2019, https://www.reuters .com/article/us-usa-trump-cnn/trump-threatens-to-sue-cnn-seeks-sub stantial-payment-over-damages-letter-idUSKBN1WX2B1.

31. Donald J. Trump (@realDonaldTrump), tweet, June 9, 2019, https:// twitter.com/realdonaldtrump/status/1137702218835136517.

32. "Former Sheriff David Clarke Temporarily Blocked from Tweeting Due to His Caustic Threats," *Wisconsin Gazette*, January 5, 2018, https://www.wisconsingazette.com/news/political/former-sheriff -david-clarke-temporarily-blocked-from-tweeting/article_3c4d0c2a -f1b0-11e7-be93-63a875edfe99.html.

33. Ryan Mac and Blake Montgomery, "Twitter Suspended Proud Boys' and Founder Gavin McInnes' Accounts Ahead of the 'Unite the Right' Rally," BuzzFeed News, August 11, 2018, https://www.buzzfeednews .com/article/ryanmac/twitter-suspends-proud-boys-and-founder -gavin-mcinnes.

34. Amy Forliti, "Actor James Woods Bashes Twitter After Getting Locked Out," Associated Press, September 23, 2018, https://apnews .com/2909e6d34b1c4d18bfac5cd186a54095.

35. Linda Givetash, "Laura Loomer Banned from Twitter After Criticizing Ilhan Omar," NBC, November 22, 2018, https://www.nbcnews.com/tech/security/laura-loomer-banned-twitter-after-criticizing-ilhan-omar-n939256.

36. Gus Garcia-Roberts, "Twitter Bans Trump-Supporting Hoaxter After USA TODAY Exposé," *USA Today*, February 26, 2019, https://www.usatoday.com/story/news/investigations/2019/02/26/jacob-wohl-spread-lies-mueller-rbg-twitter-just-banned-him/2995037002/.

37. Brian Fung, "White House Proposal Would Have FCC and FTC Police Alleged Social Media Censorship," CNN Business, August 10, 2019, https://www.cnn.com/2019/08/09/tech/white-house-social-media-executive-order-fcc-ftc/index.html.

38. McGill and Lippman, "White House Drafting Executive Order to Tackle Silicon Valley's Alleged Anti-conservative Bias."

39. Jeffrey Gottfried, Galen Stocking, and Elizabeth Grieco, "Appendix B: Political Party Detailed Tables (2016–2018)," Pew Research Center, September 25, 2018, https://www.journalism.org/2018/09/25/news-media-attitudes-appendix-b-political-party-detailed-tables/.

40. Sam Stein, "New Poll: 43% of Republicans Want to Give Trump the Power to Shut Down Media," *The Daily Beast*, August 8, 2018, https://www.thedailybeast.com/new-poll-43-of-republicans-want-to-give-trump-the-power-to-shut-down-media.

41. Bryant-Jon Anteola, "Fresno State Professor Stirs Outrage, Calls Barbara Bush an 'Amazing Racist,'" *Fresno Bee*, April 17, 2018, https://www.fresnobee.com/news/local/article209197719.html.

42. Patrick Hofstetter, "Remove Randa Jarrar from Fresno State University for Racist Comments," Change.org, 2018. https://www.change.org/p/california-state-university-remove-randa-jarrar-from-fresno-state-university-for-racist-comments.

43. Ben Shapiro, "Here's Why That Nasty Fresno State Professor Shouldn't Be Fired for Her Gross Barbara Bush Tweet," *The Daily Wire*, April 19, 2018, https://www.dailywire.com/news/29616/heres-why-nasty-fresno-state-professor-shouldnt-be-ben-shapiro.

CHAPTER 4: THE ENEMY OF DEMOCRACY

1. Donald J. Trump (@realDonaldTrump), tweet, August 2, 2019, https://twitter.com/realDonaldTrump/status/1157306452228366336.

2. Robert Mueller, "Report on the Investigation into Russian Interference in the 2016 Presidential Election," vol. 2, US Department of Justice, March 2019, https://www.justsecurity.org/wp-content/uploads/2019/04/Muelller-Report-Redacted-Vol-II-Released-04.18.2019-Word-Searchable.-Reduced-Size.pdf, 3, 44.

3. Ibid., 85, 86, 88.

4. Ibid., 114, 115–16, 118.

5. such as like Quinta Jurecic, the managing editor of Lawfare, deserve a lot of credit for isolating these incidents from the report and explaining them to the public; see Jurecic, "Obstruction of Justice in the Mueller Report: A Heat Map," Lawfare, April 21, 2019. https://www.lawfareblog.com/obstruction-justice-mueller-report-heat-map.

6. "Former Republican Federal Prosecutors Speak Out Against President Trump's Obstruction of Justice," Republicans for the Rule of Law, May 30, 2019, https://www.youtube.com/watch?v=bwnMpneFR34.

7. Ibid.

8. Donald J. Trump (@realDonaldTrump), tweet, July 9, 2019, https://twitter.com/realdonaldtrump/status/1148559443845668864.

9. Canadian Press, "'I Can't Kill These People,' Trump Says of Canadian Government as NAFTA Deadline Looms," iHeart Radio, August 31, 2018, https://www.iheartradio.ca/cjad/news/i-can-t-kill-these-people-trump-says-of-canadian-government-as-nafta-deadline-looms-1.7075888.

10. "Top Trading Partners—December 2018," United States Census Bureau, August 29, 2019, https://www.census.gov/foreign-trade/statistics/highlights/top/top1812yr.html.

11. Jim Gomez, "Rights Group Calls Duterte's Drug War Crime Against Humanity," Associated Press, July 8, 2019, https://www.apnews.com/e54b1bede70846dca1b3ba269563eba2.

12. Uri Friedman, "Turkey's Referendum: How Democracies Decline," *The Atlantic*, April 17, 2017, https://www.theatlantic.com/interna tional/archive/2017/04/turkey-referendum-democracy/523257/.

13. Susan B. Glasser, "How Trump Made War on Angela Merkel and Europe," *The New Yorker*, December 17, 2018, https://www.new yorker.com/magazine/2018/12/24/how-trump-made-war-on-angela -merkel-and-europe.

14. Julian E. Barnes and Helene Cooper, "Trump Discussed Pulling U.S. from NATO, Aides Say amid New Concerns over Russia," *New York Times*, January 14, 2019, https://www.nytimes.com/2019/01/14/us /politics/nato-president-trump.html.

15. "North Korea Profile," Freedom in the World 2018, Freedom House, https://freedomhouse.org/report/freedom-world/2018/north-korea.

16. "Report of the Commission of Inquiry on Human Rights in the Dem- ocratic People's Republic of Korea," Human Rights Council, United Nations, https://documents-dds-ny.un.org/doc/UNDOC/GEN/G14 /108/66/PDF/G1410866.pdf?OpenElement, 12.

17. Tammy Auber, "Trump Explains Kim Jong Un's Murderous Brutality: 'He's Tough,'" Mediaite, June 13, 2018, https://www.mediaite.com /tv/trump-dodges-when-confronted-on-kims-brutality-a-lot-of-other -people-have-done-bad-things-too/.

18. F. Brinley Bruton, "Trump on Otto Warmbier's Death: Kim Jong Un Wasn't to Blame," NBC News, February 28, 2019, https://www .nbcnews.com/news/world/trump-otto-warmbier-death-kim-jong-un -wasn-t-blame-n977516.

19. Donald J. Trump (@realDonaldTrump), tweet, May 25, 2019, https:// twitter.com/realDonaldTrump/status/1132459370816708608.

20. "Trump: Trump on Kim: Tough Talk . . . 'and Then We Fell in Love,'" Associated Press, September 30, 2019, https://www.apnews.com /4d56f6e8f99d4eefb2f22b7a6dd072d0.

21. Donald J. Trump (@realDonaldTrump), tweet, August 2, 2019, https:// twitter.com/realDonaldTrump/status/1157306452228366336.

22. Donald J. Trump (@realDonaldTrump), tweet, October 1, 2019, https://twitter.com/realDonaldTrump/status/1178986524630802432.

23. Nectar Gan, "Want to Escape Poverty? Replace Pictures of Jesus with Xi Jinping, Christian Villagers Urged," *South China Morning Post*, November 14, 2017, https://www.scmp.com/news/china/policies-politics /article/2119699/praise-xi-jinping-not-jesus-escape-poverty-christian.

24. Christopher Bodeen, "Group: Officials Destroying Crosses, Burning Bibles in China," Associated Press, September 10, 2018, https://www .apnews.com/c09b2ee4b71540c8a7fd6178820c5970; Chris Buckley, "China's Prisons Swell After Deluge of Arrests Engulfs Muslims," *New York Times*, August 31, 2019, https://www.nytimes.com/2019/08 /31/world/asia/xinjiang-china-uighurs-prisons.html.

25. *Congressional-Executive Commission on China—Annual Report 2018*, Congressional-Executive Commission on China, October 10, 2018, https://www.cecc.gov/sites/chinacommission.house.gov/files/docu ments/Annual%20Report%202018_2.pdf, 2.

26. "China's Xi Allowed to Remain 'President for Life' as Term Limits Removed," BBC, March 11, 2018, https://www.bbc.com/news/world -asia-china-43361276.

27. Donald J. Trump (@realDonaldTrump), tweet, August 14, 2019, https://twitter.com/realDonaldTrump/status/1161774305895694336.

28. "'They Just Kill.': Ongoing Extrajudicial Executions and Other Violations in the Philippines' 'War Against Drugs,'" Amnesty International, 2019, https://www.amnesty.org/download/Documents/ASA 3505782019ENGLISH.PDF; Matthew Tostevin and Neil Jerome Morales, "War on Numbers: Philippines Targets Drug Killing Data," Reuters, July 18, 2019, https://www.reuters.com/article/us-philip pines-drugs/war-on-numbers-philippines-targets-drug-killing-data -idUSKCN1UD1CJ.

29. "Transcript of Call Between President Trump and Philippine President Duterte," *Washington Post*, May 2, 2017, https://apps.washington post.com/g/documents/politics/transcript-of-call-between-president -trump-and-philippine-president-duterte/2446/.

30. "Turkey Country Report," Freedom in the World 2019, Freedom House, https://freedomhouse.org/report/freedom-world/2019/turkey.

31. "Remarks by President Trump and President Erdoğan of Turkey Be-

fore Bilateral Meeting," White House, September 21, 2017, https://
www.whitehouse.gov/briefings-statements/remarks-president-trump
-president-erdogan-turkey-bilateral-meeting/.

32. "Remarks by President Trump and President Erdoğan of Turkey Before Bilateral Meeting—Osaka, Japan," White House, June 29, 2019,
https://www.whitehouse.gov/briefings-statements/remarks-president
-trump-president-erdogan-turkey-bilateral-meeting-osaka-japan.

33. Joe Walsh (@WalshFreedom), tweet, July 16, 2018, https://twitter
.com/WalshFreedom/status/1018886553278525440.

34. "Remarks by President Trump and President Putin of the Russian
Federation in Joint Press Conference," White House, July 16, 2018,
https://www.whitehouse.gov/briefings-statements/remarks-president
-trump-president-putin-russian-federation-joint-press-conference/.

35. Kevin Liptak and Jeff Zeleny, "Trump, Facing Fury, Says He Mis-
spoke with Putin," CNN, July 18, 2018, https://www.cnn.com/2018
/07/17/politics/white-house-mood-donald-trump-vladimir-putin
-news-conference/index.html.

36. "Republican National Committee Resolution Supporting the Presidency of Donald J. Trump," Republican National Committee, n.d.,
https://prod-cdn-static.gop.com/media/documents/RNC_Resolution
_Supporting_the_Presidency_of_Donald_J._Trump_1549555495.pdf.

37. Zeke Miller and Steve Peoples, "Trump Campaign Takes Steps to Prevent a Challenge Within GOP," Associated Press, February 4, 2019,
https://www.apnews.com/33438efb7d794b5caf0b60f815192500.

38. Meg Kinnard, "Nevada, SC, Kansas GOP Drop Presidential Nomination Votes," Associated Press, September 7, 2019, https://apnews
.com/7e04964fc89a4312a6b410096f256add.

39. Kevin Stone, "Arizona GOP Won't Hold 2020 Presidential Preference Election," KTAR News, September 9, 2019, https://ktar.com
/story/2734796/arizona-gop-wont-hold-2020-presidential-preference
-election/.

40. James Gordon Meek and Anne Flaherty, "2nd Whistleblower Comes
Forward After Speaking with IG: Attorney," ABC News, October 6, 2019, https://abcnews.go.com/Politics/2nd-whistleblower-for

ward-speaking-ig-attorney/story?id=66092396&cid=clicksource_77
_null_bsq_hed.

41. Rebecca Klar, "Georgia GOP Submits Only Trump's Name for Primary," The Hill, December 3, 2019. https://thehill.com/homenews
/campaign/472753-georgia-gop-submits-only-trumps-name-for-pri
mary, Colin Campbell, "NC GOP Wants Its Primary Voters to Have
Only One Choice: Trump," The News & Observer, December 4, 2019.
https://www.newsobserver.com/news/politics-government/election
/article238050649.html.

CHAPTER 5: THE CULTIST

1. Paul Halsall, "Modern History Sourcebook: Hymn to Stalin," August
1997, Fordham University, https://sourcebooks.fordham.edu/mod
/stalin-worship.asp.

2. Reed Richardson, "Thanks Be to Donald: Lou Dobbs Wishes Viewers
a Great Weekend, Praises Trump for 'Making Such a Thing Possible
for Us All,'" Mediaite, September 14, 2019, https://www.mediaite.com
/tv/thanks-be-to-donald-lou-dobbs-wishes-viewers-a-great-weekend
-praises-for-trump-making-such-a-thing-possible-for-us-all/.

3. Callum Borchers, "This White House Statement on Trump's 'Positive
Energy' Reads like a Parody," Washington Post, May 30, 2017, https://
www.washingtonpost.com/news/the-fix/wp/2017/05/30/this-white
-house-statement-on-trumps-positive-energy-reads-like-a-parody/.

4. Dan Scavino Jr. (@Scavino45), tweet, August 7, 2019, https://twitter
.com/Scavino45/status/1159170408894959616.

5. "Cuomo to Trump Press Secretary: He Lies and You Know It," CNN,
August 8, 2019, https://www.cnn.com/videos/politics/2019/08/29
/cuomo-kayleigh-mcenany-trump-campaign-press-secretary-presi
dent-doesnt-lie-cpt-vpx.cnn.

6. Rebecca Morin, "RNC Chair Says Trump Primary Challengers Will
'Lose Horribly,'" Politico, February 28, 2019, https://www.politico.com
/story/2019/02/28/ronna-mcdaniel-2020-election-trump-1195652.

7. Paul Colford, "Down-to-Earth Reasons for that Heavenly Glow," As-

sociated Press, June 25, 2015, https://blog.ap.org/behind-the-news /down-to-earth-reasons-for-that-heavenly-glow.

8. Andrew Sullivan, "Andrew Sullivan on Barack Obama's Gay Marriage Evolution," *Newsweek*, May 13, 2012, https://www.newsweek.com /andrew-sullivan-barack-obamas-gay-marriage-evolution-65067.

9. David Paul Kuhn and Ben Smith, "Messianic Rhetoric Infuses Obama Rallies," *Politico*, December 9, 2007, https://www.politico.com/story /2007/12/messianic-rhetoric-infuses-obama-rallies-007281.

10. Tamara Keith, "Cabinet Members Heap Praise on Trump," NPR, June 13, 2017, https://www.npr.org/2017/06/13/532724771/cabinet -members-heap-praise-on-trump.

11. Ibid.

12. Ibid.

13. Ibid.

14. Aaron Blake, "In Cabinet Meeting, Pence Praises Trump Once Every 12 Seconds for Three Minutes Straight," *Washington Post*, December 20, 2017, https://www.washingtonpost.com/news/the-fix/wp /2017/12/20/in-cabinet-meeting-pence-praises-trump-once-every-12 -seconds-for-3-minutes-straight/.

15. John Gunther, *Inside Europe* (New York: Harper & Brothers, 1940), 516–26, https://archive.org/stream/in.ernet.dli.2015.149663/2015.14 9663.Inside-Europe#page/n537/mode/2up, 516–17.

16. CNN Transcripts, January 8, 2018, https://www.washingtonpost.com /news/politics/wp/2018/01/08/this-is-the-best-argument-to-be-made -for-trumps-political-greatness/.

17. Cheryl McHenry, Bonnie Meibers, and Thomas Gnau, "President Trump to Dayton Shooting Victim: '. . . We're with You All the Way,'" *Dayton Daily News*, August 8, 2019, https://www.daytondaily news.com/news/local/dayton-shooting-president-trump-coming-city -wednesday/V4Pvg4gNnStletCnWhC3fL/.

18. "Sen. Sherrod Brown, Dayton Mayor Nan Whaley Speak to Press on Trump's Visit," *Cincinnati Enquirer*, August 7, 2019, https://www .cincinnati.com/videos/news/2019/08/07/sen-brown-dayton-mayor -whaley-speak-press-trumps-visit/1946217001/.

19. Daniel Dale, "Fact Check: Trump Falsely Accuses Sherrod Brown, Dayton Mayor of Misrepresenting His Hospital Visit," CNN, August 7, 2019, https://www.cnn.com/2019/08/07/politics/fact-check -trump-brown-hospital-visit-dayton/index.html.

20. Dan Scavino Jr. (@Scavino45), tweet, August 7, 2019, https://twitter .com/Scavino45/status/1159170408894959616.

21. Stephanie Grisham (@PressSec), tweet, August 7, 2019, https://twit ter.com/PressSec/status/1159174708199223296.

22. Donald J. Trump (@realDonaldTrump), tweet, August 7, 2019, https://twitter.com/realdonaldtrump/status/1159189580697858048.

23. "Remarks by President Trump Before Meeting with Law Enforcement Personnel at Emergency Operations Center | El Paso, TX," White House Remarks, August 7, 2019. https://www.whitehouse.gov/brief ings-statements/remarks-president-trump-meeting-law-enforcement -personnel-emergency-operations-center-el-paso-tx/.

24. Brian Klaas, "I Study Authoritarian Despots, and Trump Is Borrow- ing a Lot of Their Tactics," Vice, January 30, 2017, https://www.vice .com/en_us/article/d7x7qx/i-study-authoritarian-despots-and-trump -is-borrowing-a-lot-of-their-tactics.

25. "Trump Gets Negative Ratings for Many Personal Traits, but Most Say He Stands Up for His Beliefs," Pew Research Center, October 1, 2019, https://www.people-press.org/2018/10/01/trump-gets-negative -ratings-for-many-personal-traits-but-most-say-he-stands-up-for-his -beliefs/.

26. "Presidential Ratings—Personal Characteristics," Gallup, https:// news.gallup.com/poll/1732/presidential-ratings-personal-characteris tics.aspx.

27. Ruth Ben-Ghiat, "Donald Trump's Cult of Personality," *HuffPost*, January 15, 2017, https://www.huffpost.com/entry/donald-trumps -cult-of-per_b_8992650.

28. "Republicans Now Are More Open to the Idea of Expanding Presi- dential Power," Pew Research Center, August 7, 2019, https://www .people-press.org/2019/08/07/republicans-now-are-more-open-to-the -idea-of-expanding-presidential-power/.

29. Joe Walsh (@WalshFreedom), tweet, May 5, 2019, https://twitter.com /WalshFreedom/status/1125131891965878276.

30. Rush Limbaugh, "Why We Must Hang with Trump on Tariffs," iHeart Radio, May 13, 2019, https://news.iheart.com/featured/rush -limbaugh/content/2019-05-13-rush-limbaugh-blog-why-we-must -hang-with-trump-on-tariffs/.

31. Thom Tillis, "I Support Trump's Vision on Border Security. But I Would Vote Against the Emergency," *Washington Post*, February 25, 2019, https://www.washingtonpost.com/opinions/2019/02 /25/i-support-trumps-vision-border-security-i-would-vote-against -emergency/.

32. Brian Murphy, "Tillis Reverses Course, Votes to Support Trump on National Emergency Declaration," *Charlotte Observer*, March 14, 2019, https://www.charlotteobserver.com/news/politics-government /article227742754.html.

33. "Read the Unclassified Version of the Whistleblower complaint Against Trump, CBS News, September 26, 2019. https://www.cbsnews.com /news/whistleblower-complaint-full-text-read-the-unclassified-ver sion-of-the-whistleblower-complaint-against-president/.

34. Patrick Reevell and Lucien Bruggeman, "Ukrainians Understood Biden Probe Was Condition for Trump-Zelenskiy Talks, Says Former Ukrainian Adviser," ABC News, September 25, 2019, https://abc news.go.com/Politics/ukrainians-understood-biden-probe-condition -trump-zelenskiy-phone/story?id=65863043.

35. John Santucci, Alexander Mallin, Pierre Thomas, and Katherine Faulders, "Trump Urged Ukraine to Work with Barr and Giuliani to Probe Biden: Call Transcript," ABC News, September 25, 2019, https:// abcnews.go.com/Politics/transcript-trump-call-ukraine-includes-talk -giuliani-barr/story?id=65848768.

36. Ibid.

37. Joe Walsh (@WalshFreedom), tweet, September 26, 2019, https:// twitter.com/WalshFreedom/status/1177213462017171458.

38. Andrew P. Bakaj, "RE: Safety Concerns Regarding the Intelligence Community Whistleblower," Compass Rose Legal Group, Septem-

ber 28, 2019, https://compassrosepllc.com/wp-content/uploads/2019
/09/2019_0928_-Correspondence-to-DNI.pdf.

39. "Trump: 'Trying to Find Out' Whistleblower Identity," Associated
Press, YouTube, September 30, 2019, https://www.youtube.com
/watch?v=r-7L-eRBNAk.

40. Donald J. Trump (@realDonaldTrump), tweet, October 1, 2019,
https://twitter.com/realDonaldTrump/status/1179023004241727489.

41. Tom Jacobs, "A Cult Expert Finds Familiar Patterns of Behavior in
Trump's GOP," *Pacific Standard*, June 21, 2018, https://psmag.com/news
/a-sociologist-explains-the-similarities-between-cults-and-trumps-gop.

42. Jason Lemon, "'At Least Two Dozen' Republicans in House Are
'Deeply Concerned' About Trump's Ukraine Actions: Congressman,"
Newsweek, October 6, 2019, https://www.newsweek.com/least-two
-dozen-republicans-house-deeply-concerned-trump-ukraine-con
gressman-1463427.

43. Mariam Khan, "GOP Senators Critical of President Trump over
Ukraine Dealings, Syria," ABC News, October 21, 2019, https://abc
news.go.com/Politics/gop-senators-critical-president-trump-ukraine
-dealings-syria/story?id=66417302.

44. "'This Week' Transcript 11-3-19: Mayor Pete Buttigieg, Rep. Eliot
Engel, Rep. Steve Scalise," ABC News, November 3, 2019, https://
abcnews.go.com/Politics/week-transcript-11-19-mayor-pete-buttigieg
-rep/story?id=66721987.

CHAPTER 6: THE NARCISSIST

1. He referred to himself alternatively as "John Miller" and "John Bar-
ron"; see Marc Fisher and Will Hobson, "Donald Trump Masquer-
aded as Publicist to Brag About Himself," *Washington Post*, May 13,
2016, https://www.washingtonpost.com/politics/donald-trump-alter
-ego-barron/2016/05/12/02ac99ec-16fe-11e6-aa55-670cabef46e0
_story.html?asdfk.

2. "Republican Presidential Politics," C-SPAN, July 14, 2016, https://
www.c-span.org/video/?412218-3/washington-journal-peter-wehner
-republican-party-campaign-2016.

3. George T. Conway III, "Unfit for Office," *The Atlantic*, October 3, 2019, https://www.theatlantic.com/ideas/archive/2019/10/george-con way-trump-unfit-office/599128/.
4. Donald J. Trump (@realDonaldTrump), tweet, October 7, 2019, https://twitter.com/realDonaldTrump/status/1181232249821388801.
5. Aaron Blake, "President Trump's Full Washington Post Interview Transcript, Annotated," *Washington Post*, November 27, 2018, https:// www.washingtonpost.com/politics/2018/11/27/president-trumps-full -washington-post-interview-transcript-annotated/?noredirect=on.
6. Conway, "Unfit for Office."
7. Ibid.
8. Lori Robertson, "Factcheck: Adam Schiff's 'Parody' and President Trump's Response," *USA Today*, November 13, 2019. https:// www.usatoday.com/story/news/politics/2019/11/13/impeaching -hearing-factcheck-adam-schiff-parody/4178449002/.
9. Ed Morrissey, "Stephanopoulos to Schiff: If What Trump Said Was So Bad, Why Make Up Dialogue?," Hot Air, September 30, 2019, https://hotair.com/archives/ed-morrissey/2019/09/30/stephanopoulos -schiff-trump-said-bad-make-dialogue/.
10. Donald J. Trump, tweet, September 30, 2019, https://twitter.com/real DonaldTrump/status/1178643854737772545.
11. "Remarks by President Trump and President Niinistö of the Republic of Finland Before Bilateral Meeting," White House Remarks, October 2, 2019. https://www.whitehouse.gov/briefings-statements/remarks-presi dent-trump-president-niinisto-republic-finland-bilateral-meeting/.
12. Erica Payne, "Granny off the Cliff Part 2," YouTube, August 11, 2012, https://www.youtube.com/watch?v=hrdeyMNZW88.
13. Eli Stokols, "Listen: Audio of Trump Discussing Whistleblower at Private Event: 'That's Close to a Spy,'" *Los Angeles Times*, September 26, 2019, https://www.latimes.com/politics/story/2019-09-26 /trump-at-private-breakfast-who-gave-the-whistle-blower-the-infor mation-because-thats-almost-a-spy.
14. Masha Gessen, "Donald Trump's Very Soviet Fixation on Applause," *The New Yorker*, February 6, 2018, https://www.newyorker.com/news /our-columnists/donald-trumps-very-soviet-fixation-on-applause.

15. "Read the Trump-Ukraine Phone Call Readout," Politico, September 25, 2019. https://www.politico.com/story/2019/09/25/trump-ukraine -phone-call-transcript-text-pdf-1510770.

16. "Transcript: ABC News' George Stephanopoulos' Exclusive Interview with President Trump," ABC News, June 16, 2019, https://abcnews .go.com/Politics/transcript-abc-news-george-stephanopoulos-exclu sive-interview-president/story?id=63749144.

17. Pilar Melendez, "Trump: 'China Should Start an Investigation into the Bidens,'" *The Daily Beast*, October 3, 2019, https://www.thedaily beast.com/trump-china-should-start-an-investigation-into-the -bidens.

18. N. Gregory Mankiw, "Economists Actually Agree on This: The Wisdom of Free Trade," *New York Times*, April 24, 2015, https://www .nytimes.com/2015/04/26/upshot/economists-actually-agree-on-this -point-the-wisdom-of-free-trade.html?mcubz=0.

CHAPTER 7: FIXING THE PRESIDENCY

1. Tim Alberta, *American Carnage: On the Front Lines of the Republican Civil War and the Rise of President Trump* (New York: Harper, 2019), 347.

2. Tucker Higgins, "Nancy Pelosi Warns GOP That a Democratic President Could Declare Gun Violence a National Emergency," CNBC, February 14, 2019, https://www.cnbc.com/2019/02/14/pelosi-warns -gop-that-a-democratic-president-could-declare-a-national-emer gency-on-guns.html; Benjy Sarlin, "Tom Steyer: I'll Declare a National Emergency to Tackle Climate Change," NBC News, October 18, 2019, https://www.nbcnews.com/politics/meet-the-press /blog/meet-press-blog-latest-news-analysis-data-driving-political -discussion-n988541/ncrd1034801#blogHeader.

3. Ben Watson, "US Customs Officer Harasses Defense One Journalist at Dulles Airport," Defense One, October 4, 2019, https://www.de fenseone.com/threats/2019/10/us-customs-officer-harasses-defense -one-journalist-dulles/160380/.

4. Jonathan Chait, "Trump Directs Government to Punish *Washington Post* Owner," New York Intelligencer, August 2, 2019, http://nymag

.com/intelligencer/2019/08/trump-punish-amazon-washington-post
-owner-jeff-bezos.html.

5. "50 States and Territories Projects," NPR, https://apps.npr.org
/documents/document.html?id=6382249-50-States-and-Territories
-Projects.

6. Mike Lee, "Sen. Lee Introduces ARTICLE ONE Act to Reclaim
Congressional Power," March 12, 2019, https://www.lee.senate.gov
/public/index.cfm/2019/3/sen-lee-introduces-article-one-act-to-re
claim-congressional-power.

7. Donald F. McGahn II, "Memorandum to All White House Staff,"
January 27, 2017, *Politico*, https://www.politico.com/f/?id=0000015a
-dde8-d23c-a7ff-dfef4d530000.

8. Rebecca Jones, "The Dangers of Chronic Federal Vacancies," Project
on Government Oversight, August 6, 2019, https://www.pogo.org
/analysis/2019/08/the-dangers-of-chronic-federal-vacancies/.

9. Michael Crowley and Tyler Pager, "Trump Urges Russia to Hack
Clinton's Email," *Politico*, July 27, 2016, https://www.politico.com
/story/2016/07/trump-putin-no-relationship-226282.

10. Melanie Arter, "Trump to Ukraine: 'There's a Lot of Talk About Biden's
Son, That Biden Stopped the Prosecution,'" CBS News, September 25, 2019, https://www.cnsnews.com/news/article/melanie-arter
/trump-ukraine-theres-lot-talk-about-bidens-son-biden-stopped
-prosecution.

11. Kevin Breuninger, "Trump Says China Should Investigate the Bidens,
Doubles Down on Ukraine Probe," CNBC, October 3, 2019, https://
www.cnbc.com/2019/10/03/trump-calls-for-ukraine-china-to-inves
tigate-the-bidens.html.

12. "Transcript: ABC News' George Stephanopoulos' Exclusive Interview
with President Trump," ABC News, June 16, 2019, https://abcnews
.go.com/Politics/transcript-abc-news-george-stephanopoulos-exclu
sive-interview-president/story?id=63749144.

13. Morgan Phillips, "Trump Scraps Plans to Host 2020 G-7 Summit
at Doral Resort amid Dem Uproar," Fox News, October 20, 2019,
https://www.foxnews.com/politics/trump-doral-resort-out-2020-g7
-summit.

14. 5 US Code, section 3110, "Employment of Relatives; Restrictions," December 16, 1967, https://www.law.cornell.edu/uscode/text/5/3110.
15. David Shepardson, "Trump Praises Chinese President Extending Tenure 'for Life,'" March 3, 2018, https://www.reuters.com/article/us -trump-china/trump-praises-chinese-president-extending-tenure-for -life-idUSKCN1GG015.
16. Donald J. Trump (@realDonaldTrump), tweet, August 21, 2019, https://twitter.com/realDonaldTrump/status/1164138796205654016.
17. David Mack (@davidmackau), tweet, August 21, 2019, https://twitter .com/davidmackau/status/1164217774564159488.

CHAPTER 8: FIXING CONSERVATISM

1. Colin Dwyer, "Donald Trump: 'I Could . . . Shoot Somebody, and I Wouldn't Lose Any Voters,'" NPR, January 23, 2016, https://www .npr.org/sections/thetwo-way/2016/01/23/464129029/donald-trump -i-could-shoot-somebody-and-i-wouldnt-lose-any-voters.
2. Jennifer Jacobs (@JenniferJJacobs), tweet, July 15, 2019, https://twitter .com/JenniferJJacobs/status/1150911765699579904.
3. Donald J. Trump (@realDonaldTrump), tweet, October 7, 2019, https://twitter.com/realdonaldtrump/status/1181232249821388801.
4. Judd Gregg, "Judd Gregg: Trump Is the Almost, Occasionally, Pretty Close to Socialist Policy Guy," The Hill, September 16, 2019, https:// thehill.com/opinion/campaign/461505-judd-gregg-trump-is-the-al most-occasionally-pretty-close-to-socialist-policy.
5. Joshua Gillin, "Bush Says Trump Was a Democrat Longer than a Re- publican 'in the Last Decade,'" PolitiFact, August 24, 2015, https:// www.politifact.com/florida/statements/2015/aug/24/jeb-bush/bush -says-trump-was-democrat-longer-republican-las/.
6. Phil Hirschkorn, "Trump Proposes Massive One-Time Tax on the Rich," CNN, November 9, 1999, https://www.cnn.com/ALLPOLI TICS/stories/1999/11/09/trump.rich/index.html?_s=PM:ALL POLITICS.
7. Philip Bump, "Donald Trump Took 5 Different Positions on Abortion

in 3 Days," *Washington Post*, April 3, 2016, https://www.washington
post.com/news/the-fix/wp/2016/04/03/donald-trumps-ever-shifting
-positions-on-abortion/.

8. Donald J. Trump (@realDonaldTrump), tweet, November 13, 2012,
https://twitter.com/realdonaldtrump/status/268431151666954241.

9. Donald J. Trump (@realDonaldTrump), tweet, January 13, 2012,
https://twitter.com/realDonaldTrump/status/157918533655871488.

10. Donald J. Trump (@realDonaldTrump), tweet, September 7, 2019,
https://twitter.com/realdonaldtrump/status/1170469618177236992.

11. Donald J. Trump (@realDonaldTrump), tweet, June 4, 2014, https://
twitter.com/realdonaldtrump/status/474134260149157888/?.

12. Gregg, "Judd Gregg: Trump Is the Almost, Occasionally, Pretty Close
to Socialist Policy Guy."

13. Phyllis Schlafly, *The Conservative Case for Trump* (Washington, DC:
Regnery, 2016).

14. Donald J. Trump, "Remarks by President Trump at the Conservative Political Action Conference," White House, February 23, 2018,
https://www.whitehouse.gov/briefings-statements/remarks-president
-trump-conservative-political-action-conference-2/.

15. "'This Week' Transcript: Hillary Clinton, Sen. Bernie Sanders and
Donald Trump," ABC News, January 31, 2016, https://abcnews.go
.com/Politics/week-transcript-hillary-clinton-sen-bernie-sanders
-donald/story?id=36619138.

16. "Republican Candidates Debate in Houston, Texas," American Presidency Project, February 25, 2016, https://www.presidency.ucsb.edu
/documents/republican-candidates-debate-houston-texas.

17. Ibid.

18. Kevin Liptak, "Trump: 'Nobody Knew Health Care Could Be So
Complicated,'" CNN, February 28, 2017, https://www.cnn.com/2017
/02/27/politics/trump-health-care-complicated/index.html.

19. Donald J. Trump (@realDonaldTrump), tweet, March 26, 2019,
https://twitter.com/realdonaldtrump/status/1110586787808903168.

20. Alex Wayne (@aawayne), tweet, March 26, 2019, https://twitter.com
/aawayne/status/1110613053404602370.

21. Judy Woodruff, "George Will on American Conservatism and Trump's 'Lasting Damage,'" *PBS NewsHour*, July 22, 2019, https://www.pbs.org/newshour/show/george-will-on-american-conservatism -and-trumps-lasting-damage.

22. Ezra Klein, "George Will Makes the Conservative Case Against Democracy," *Vox*, July 18, 2019. https://www.vox.com/ezra-klein -show-podcast/2019/7/18/20698397/george-will-conservative-sens ibility-republicans-donald-trump.

23. Mark Muro, Robert Maxim, and Jacob Whiton, "Automation and Artificial Intelligence: How Machines Are Affecting People and Places," Brookings Institution, January 24, 2019, https://www.brookings.edu /research/automation-and-artificial-intelligence-how-machines-affect -people-and-places/.

CHAPTER 9: FIXING THE DEBT

1. Bob Woodward and Robert Costa, "Transcript: Donald Trump Interview with Bob Woodward and Robert Costa," *Washington Post*, April 2, 2016, https://www.washingtonpost.com/news/post-poli tics/wp/2016/04/02/transcript-donald-trump-interview-with-bob -woodward-and-robert-costa/.

2. Stephen Gandel, "Donald Trump in His Own Words: Atlantic City to the White House," *Fortune*, April 21, 2016, https://fortune.com/2016 /04/21/donald-trump-q-and-a/.

3. Woodward and Costa, "Transcript: Donald Trump Interview with Bob Woodward and Robert Costa."

4. "Remarks by President Trump, President Moon, Commerce Secretary Ross, and NEC Director Cohn in Bilateral Meeting," White House Remarks, https://www.whitehouse.gov/briefings-statements/remarks -president-trump-president-moon-commerce-secretary-ross-nec-di rector-cohn-bilateral-meeting/.

5. "Did the Trade Deficit Cause $20 Trillion in Debt?," Committee for a Responsible Federal Budget, July 6, 2017, https://www.crfb.org/blogs /did-trade-deficit-cause-20-trillion-debt.

6. Marin Cogan, "GOP Frosh: Obama Budget a 'Joke,'" *Politico*, Feb-

ruary 14, 2011, https://www.politico.com/story/2011/02/gop-frosh
-obama-budget-a-joke-049481.

7. "The CBS News Republican Debate Transcript, Annotated," *Washington Post*, February 13, 2016, https://www.washingtonpost.com
/news/the-fix/wp/2016/02/13/the-cbs-republican-debate-transcript
-annotated/.

8. Social Security and Medicare Boards of Trustees, "A Summary of the
2019 Annual Reports," Social Security Administration, https://www
.ssa.gov/oact/TRSUM/.

9. "Gross Domestic Product, Fourth Quarter and Annual 2018 (Initial
Estimate)," Bureau of Economic Analysis, U.S. Department of Commerce, February 28, 2019, https://www.bea.gov/news/2019/initial
-gross-domestic-product-4th-quarter-and-annual-2018.

10. Asawin Suebsaeng and Lachlan Markay, "Trump on Coming Debt
Crisis: 'I Won't Be Here' When It Blows Up," *The Daily Beast*,
March 14, 2019, https://www.thedailybeast.com/trump-on-coming
-debt-crisis-i-wont-be-here-when-it-blows-up.

11. "Fix the National Debt," Committee for a Responsible Federal Budget, http://www.crfb.org/debtfixer/.

12. Social Security and Medicare Boards of Trustees, "A Summary of the
2019 Annual Reports."

13. Suebsaeng and Markay, "Trump on Coming Debt Crisis: 'I Won't Be
Here' When It Blows Up."

14. Ibid.

15. House Freedom Caucus (@freedom caucus), tweet, February 7, 2018,
https://twitter.com/freedomcaucus/status/961398045022871552.

16. Eliza Collins, "As Paul Ryan Turns to Democrats for Votes, Conservatives Fume over Budget Deal," *USA Today*, February 8, 2018,
https://www.usatoday.com/story/news/politics/2018/02/08/paul
-ryan-turns-democrats-votes-conservatives-fume-over-budget-deal
/320248002/.

17. Mark Meadows, "House Freedom Caucus Opposes Budget Agreement," July 23, 2019, https://meadows.house.gov/news/document
single.aspx?DocumentID=3058.

18. Ramsey Touchberry, "23 Senate Republicans Break with Don-

ald Trump over Massive Budget Deal," *Newsweek*, August 1, 2019, https://www.newsweek.com/republicans-rebuke-massive-trump-backed-budget-deal-measure-passes-1452139.

19. Donald J. Trump (@realDonaldTrump), tweet, August 1, 2019. https://twitter.com/realdonaldtrump/status/1156935288322699265?lang=en.

20. "POTUS Rescission Transmittal Package," White House, https://www.whitehouse.gov/wp-content/uploads/2018/05/POTUS-Rescission-Transmittal-Package-5.8.2018.pdf.

21. Michelle Lee, "Fact Check: Has Trump Declared Bankruptcy Four or Six Times?," *Washington Post*, September 26, 2016, https://www.washingtonpost.com/politics/2016/live-updates/general-election/real-time-fact-checking-and-analysis-of-the-first-presidential-debate/fact-check-has-trump-declared-bankruptcy-four-or-six-times/.

CHAPTER 10: FIXING TRADE

1. Donald Trump, "The America We Deserve," (Los Angeles: Renaissance Books, 2000). https://books.google.com/books?id=PV6qZU_xev8C&q=world+war+II#v=snippet&q=enemies%20in%20world%20war%20II&f=false.

2. Donald J. Trump, *Time to Get Tough: Make America Great Again!* (Washington D.C.: Regnery Publishing, 2011), 31.

3. Dylan Matthews, "Zero-Sum Trump," Vox, January 19, 2017, https://www.vox.com/a/donald-trump-books.

4. "Section 201 Cases: Imported Large Residential Washing Machines and Imported Solar Cells and Modules," Office of the United States Trade Representative, https://ustr.gov/sites/default/files/files/Press/fs/201%20FactSheet.pdf.

5. "Public Law 87-794," US Government Printing Office, October 11, 1962, https://www.govinfo.gov/content/pkg/STATUTE-76/pdf/STATUTE-76-Pg872.pdf, 872; "Presidential Proclamation on Adjusting Imports of Steel into the United States," White House, March 8, 2018, https://www.whitehouse.gov/presidential-actions/presidential-proclamation-adjusting-imports-steel-united-states/;

"Presidential Proclamation on Adjusting Imports of Aluminum into the United States," White House, March 8, 2018, https://www.white house.gov/presidential-actions/presidential-proclamation-adjusting -imports-aluminum-united-states/.

6. "What You Need to Know About Implementing Steel and Aluminum Tariffs on Canada, Mexico, and the European Union," White House, May 31, 2018, https://www.whitehouse.gov/articles/need-know-im plementing-steel-aluminum-tariffs-canada-mexico-european-union/.

7. "Trade Act of 1974," US House of Representatives, August 6, 2018, https://legcounsel.house.gov/Comps/93-618.pdf, 195, 191.

8. Donald J. Trump, "Statement by the President Regarding Trade with China," White House, June 15, 2018, https://www.whitehouse.gov /briefings-statements/statement-president-regarding-trade-china/.

9. Donald J. Trump, "Statement from the President," White House, September 17, 2018, https://www.whitehouse.gov/briefings-statements /statement-from-the-president-4/.

10. "Statement by U.S. Trade Representative Robert Lighthizer on Section 301 Action," Office of the United States Trade Representative, May 10, 2019, https://ustr.gov/about-us/policy-offices/press-office /press-releases/2019/may/statement-us-trade-representative.

11. Caitlain Devereaux Lewis, "Presidential Authority over Trade: Imposing Tariffs and Duties," Congressional Research Service, December 9, 2016, https://fas.org/sgp/crs/misc/R44707.pdf, 1.

12. Erica York, Kyle Pomerleau, and Scott Eastman, "Tracking the Economic Impact of U.S. Tariffs and Retaliatory Actions," Tax Foundation, May 31, 2019, https://taxfoundation.org/tariffs-trump-trade -war/.

13. Rick Newman, "Trump's Trade War Has Killed 300,000 Jobs," Yahoo! Finance, September 10, 2019, https://finance.yahoo.com/news /trumps-trade-war-has-killed-300000-jobs-194717808.html.

14. Dion Rabouin, "Trump's Trade War Is Being Felt Throughout the Economy," Axios, September 12, 2019, https://www.axios.com /trumps-trade-war-is-being-felt-throughout-the-economy-cf192439 -cd83-4bfa-a9b8-a28e4659d8b1.html.

15. "2019 Footwear Tariff Letter," Footwear Distributors and Retailers of America, May 20, 2019, https://fdra.org/wp-content/uploads/2019/05/2019-Footwear-Tariff-Letter-1.pdf.
16. Mary Catherine Wellons, "The $400 Billion Outdoor Industry Sounds Alarm on Trump's Trade War Tariffs," CNBC, September 13, 2019, https://www.cnbc.com/2019/09/13/the-400-billion-outdoor-industry-sounds-alarm-on-trumps-trade-war.html.
17. Richard Waters, "How the Trade War Is Damaging the US Tech Industry," *Financial Times*, August 15, 2019, https://www.ft.com/content/16fa93ba-bf69-11e9-b350-db00d509634e.
18. "China Trade Standstill More Bad News for Farmers," American Farm Bureau Federation, August 5, 2019, https://www.fb.org/newsroom/china-trade-standstill-more-bad-news-for-farmers.
19. "China: Top Market for U.S. Ag Exports," Minnesota Department of Agriculture, https://www.mda.state.mn.us/sites/default/files/inline-files/profilechina.pdf.
20. Kamron Daugherty and Hui Jiang, "Outlook for U.S. Agricultural Trade," United States Department of Agriculture, May 30, 2019, https://www.ers.usda.gov/webdocs/publications/93215/aes-108.pdf?v=5416.2.
21. Bloomberg TicToc (@tictoc), tweet, March 2, 2018, https://twitter.com/i/moments/969519906097106944?lang=en.
22. "Farm Policy: USDA's 2018 Trade Aid Package," Homeland Security Digital Library, June 19, 2019, https://www.hsdl.org/?abstract&did=826586.
23. "USDA Announces Support for Farmers Impacted by Unjustified Retaliation and Trade Disruption," U.S. Department of Agriculture, May 23, 2019, https://www.usda.gov/media/press-releases/2019/05/23/usda-announces-support-farmers-impacted-unjustified-retaliation-and.
24. Ibid.
25. Donald J. Trump (@realDonaldTrump), tweet, May 10, 2019, https://twitter.com/realdonaldtrump/status/1126833126179840000.
26. "China—Agricultural Industry," International Trade Administration,

July 30, 2019, https://www.export.gov/article?id=China-Agricultural
-Sectors.

27. Donald J. Trump (@realDonaldTrump), tweet, May 10, 2019, https://
twitter.com/realdonaldtrump/status/1126815126584266753?lang=en.

28. Nahal Toosi, "Trump Plan Would Steer Foreign Aid to 'Friends and
Allies,'" *Politico*, September 6, 2019, https://www.politico.com/story
/2019/09/06/trump-foreign-aid-allies-1483788.

29. Donald J. Trump (@realDonaldTrump), tweet, July 23, 2019, https://
twitter.com/realdonaldtrump/status/1153634372442107904.

30. Alan Rappeport, "Farmers' Frustration with Trump Grows as U.S.
Escalates China Fight," *New York Times*, August 27, 2019, https://
www.nytimes.com/2019/08/27/us/politics/trump-farmers-china
-trade.html. During that same forum, Perdue joked, "What do you
call two farmers in a basement? A whine cellar."

31. Alan Rappeport, "U.S. Rolls Out More Farm Aid as Soy Growers
Urge Trade Cease-Fire," *New York Times*, July 25, 2019, https://www
.nytimes.com/2019/07/25/us/politics/farm-aid-trade-wars.html.

32. Steve Karnowski and Balint Szalai, "Some Big Farms Collect Big
Checks from Trump Aid Package," Associated Press, July 3, 2019,
https://www.apnews.com/c40f92fefbac487fb2a0bb8f9a5b6643.

33. James MacPherson, "Economist: New Trump Farm Aid May Be Dis-
tributed More Fairly," Associated Press, July 26, 2019, https://www
.apnews.com/c753b1f7330443728dc5e4cc8b7be2dd.

34. "USDA Announces Support for Farmers Impacted by Unjustified Retaliation and Trade Disruption," US Department of Agriculture, May 23,
2019, https://www.usda.gov/media/press-releases/2019/05/23/usda-an
nounces-support-farmers-impacted-unjustified-retaliation-and.

35. P. J. Huffstutter, "Trump Trade-War Aid Sows Frustration in Farm
Country," Reuters, September 13, 2019, https://www.reuters.com
/article/us-usa-trade-china-aid/trump-trade-war-aid-sows-frustra
tion-in-farm-country-idUSKCN1VY0ZT.

36. Alan Rappeport, "Peter Navarro Invented an Expert for His Books,
Based on Himself," *New York Times*, October 16, 2019, https://www
.nytimes.com/2019/10/16/us/politics/peter-navarro-ron-vara.html.

37. Tom Bartlett, "Trump's 'China Muse' Has an Imaginary Friend," *The Chronicle of Higher Education*, October 15, 2019, https://www.chroni cle.com/interactives/20191015-navarro.

38. Scott Horsley, "White House Adviser Peter Navarro Calls Fictional Alter Ego an 'Inside Joke,'" NPR, October 18, 2019, https://www.npr .org/2019/10/18/771396016/white-house-adviser-peter-navarro-calls -fictional-alter-ego-an-inside-joke.

39. Bob Sellers, "Tariff Man: Behind Trump Economic Advisor Peter Navarro's Long Quest to Ratchet Up the Trade War with China," *Fortune*, August 27, 2019, https://fortune.com/2019/08/27/tariff -man-behind-trump-economic-advisor-peter-navarros-long-quest-to -ratchet-up-the-trade-war-with-china/.

40. Josh Dawsey and Damian Paletta, "'My Peter': Rising Influence of Controversial Trump Trade Adviser Navarro Concerns His Critics," *Washington Post*, June 12, 2019, https://www.washingtonpost.com /politics/my-peter-rising-influence-of-controversial-trump-trade-ad viser-navarro-concerns-his-critics/2019/06/12/e4fcb81c-8b96-11e9 -b162-8f6f41ec3c04_story.html.

41. Melissa Chan, "Trump's Top China Expert Isn't a China Expert," *Foreign Policy*, March 13, 2017, https://foreignpolicy.com/2017/03/13 /peter-navarro-profile-national-trade-council-donald-trump-china -expert/.

42. Annie Lowrey, "The 'Madman' Behind Trump's Trade Theory," *The Atlantic*, December 2018, https://www.theatlantic.com/magazine/ar chive/2018/12/peter-navarro-trump-trade/573913/.

CHAPTER 11: FIXING IMMIGRATION

1. *Politico* (@politico), tweet, January 10, 2019, https://twitter.com/po litico/status/1083448877666193409.

2. Michelle Hackman, "U.S. Immigration Courts' Backlog Exceeds One Million Cases," *Wall Street Journal*, September 18, 2019, https://www .wsj.com/articles/u-s-immigration-courts-backlog-exceeds-one-mil lion-cases-11568845885.

3. Barack Obama, *The Audacity of Hope: Thoughts on Reclaiming the American Dream* (New York: Crown Publishers, 2006), 268.

4. Fact Checker, "In 993 Days, President Trump has Made 13,435 False or Misleading Claims," *Washington Post*, October 9, 2019, https://www.washingtonpost.com/graphics/politics/trump-claims-database/.

5. Donald J. Trump (@realDonaldTrump), tweet, July 14, 2019, https://twitter.com/realDonaldTrump/status/1150381395078000643.

6. Z. Byron Wolf, "Trump's Attacks on Judge Curiel Are Still Jarring to Read," CNN, February 27, 2018, https://www.cnn.com/2018/02/27/politics/judge-curiel-trump-border-wall/index.html.

7. "Remarks by President Trump and President Mattarella of the Italian Republic Before Bilateral Meeting," White House, October 16, 2019, https://www.whitehouse.gov/briefings-statements/remarks-president-trump-president-mattarella-italian-republic-bilateral-meeting/.

8. This specific wording came from a rally in San Jose on June 2, 2016; see Miriam Valverde, "Donald Trump Stalls on Promise to Build a Wall, Have Mexico Pay for It," PolitiFact, January 14, 2019, https://www.politifact.com/truth-o-meter/promises/trumpometer/promise/1397/build-wall-and-make-mexico-pay-it/.

9. "Homeland Security Secretary Confirmation Hearing," C-SPAN, January 10, 2017, https://www.c-span.org/video/?421234-1/homeland-security-nominee-general-john-kelly-testifies-confirmation-hearing.

10. "Written Testimony of DHS Secretary John F. Kelly for a Senate Committee on Homeland Security and Governmental Affairs Hearing Titled 'Improving Border Security and Public Safety,'" US Department of Homeland Security, April 5, 2017, https://www.dhs.gov/news/2017/04/05/written-testimony-dhs-secretary-kelly-senate-committee-homeland-security-and.

11. Donald Judd, "Kelly Dismisses Need for Wall Along Full U.S. Mexico Border," CNN, March 7, 2019, https://www.cnn.com/2019/03/07/politics/john-kelly-border-wall/index.html.

12. Jerry Markon and Dan Lamothe, "Retired Marine Gen. John Kelly Picked to Head Homeland Security," *Washington Post*, December 7, 2016, https://www.washingtonpost.com/world/national-security/re

tired-marine-gen-john-f-kelly-picked-to-head-department-of-home
land-security/2016/12/07/165472f2-bbe6-11e6-94ac-3d324840106c
_story.html.

13. Franco Ordoñez, "Trump Pick to Head Homeland Security Oversaw
Guantánamo Prison," McClatchy, December 7, 2016, https://www
.mcclatchydc.com/news/nation-world/national/article119427068
.html.

14. "Public Law 115-31—May 5, 2017," US Congress, https://www.con
gress.gov/115/plaws/publ31/PLAW-115publ31.pdf.

15. "Consolidated Appropriations Act, 2018," US Congress. https://www
.congress.gov/115/plaws/publ141/PLAW-115publ141.pdf.

16. "Consolidated Appropriations Act, 2019," US Congress, https://con
gress.gov/116/bills/hjres31/BILLS-116hjres31enr.pdf.

17. Laura Meckler, "Trump Administration Seeks $18 Billion over De-
cade to Expand Border Wall," *Wall Street Journal*, January 5, 2018,
https://www.wsj.com/articles/trump-administration-seeks-18-billion
-over-decade-to-expand-border-wall-1515148381.

18. "H.R. 7059–Build the Wall, Enforce the Law Act of 2018," US Congress, October 12, 2018, https://www.congress.gov/bill/115th-congress
/house-bill/7059/text.

19. Burgess Everett and Seung Min Kim, "Schumer Withdraws Offer on
Trump's Wall," *Politico*, January 23, 2018, https://www.politico.com
/story/2018/01/23/chuck-schumer-trump-wall-offer-359156.

20. Brandon Carter, "50 States and Territories Projects," NPR, https://
apps.npr.org/documents/document.html?id=6382249-50-States-and
-Territories-Projects.

21. Paul Sonne, "To Pay for Trump's Wall, a Hurricane-Wrecked Base
in Puerto Rico Loses Funding," *Washington Post*, September 19,
2019, https://www.washingtonpost.com/world/national-security
/at-half-ruined-puerto-rico-base-hurricane-recovery-funds-pulled-for
-trumps-wall/2019/09/19/173ad4f4-d63c-11e9-ab26-e6dbebac45d3
_story.html.

22. Lamar Alexander, "Alexander Statement on Vote to Disapprove of
National Emergency Declaration," September 25, 2019, https://www

.alexander.senate.gov/public/index.cfm/2019/9/alexander-statement -on-vote-to-disapprove-of-national-emergency-declaration.

23. Tim Lau, "Progress Toward Reforming the National Emergencies Act," Brennan Center for Justice, July 29, 2019, https://www.brennan center.org/our-work/analysis-opinion/progress-toward-reforming-na tional-emergencies-act.

24. Pete Williams, "Judge Rules Trump Violated the Law on Wall Funding with National Emergency," NBC News, October 11, 2019, https:// www.nbcnews.com/politics/immigration/judge-rules-trump-violated -law-wall-funding-national-emergency-n1065216.

25. Nick Miroff and Josh Dawsey, "'Take the Land': President Trump Wants a Border Wall. He Wants It Black. And He Wants It by Election Day," *Washington Post*, August 27, 2019, https://www.wash ingtonpost.com/immigration/take-the-land-president-trump -wants-a-border-wall-he-wants-it-black-and-he-wants-it-by-elec tion-day/2019/08/27/37b80018-c821-11e9-a4f3-c081a126de70 _story.html.

26. Salvador Rizzo, "More Than Two Years Later, Trump's Wall Remains Unbuilt," *Washington Post*, September 6, 2019, https://www.washing tonpost.com/politics/2019/09/06/more-than-two-years-later-trumps -wall-remains-unbuilt/.

27. Donald J. Trump, "Remarks by President Trump in Meeting on Human Trafficking on the Southern Border," White House, February 1, 2019, https://www.whitehouse.gov/briefings-statements/remarks-president -trump-meeting-human-trafficking-southern-border/.

28. Donald J. Trump (@realDonaldTrump), tweet, January 2, 2019, https://twitter.com/realDonaldTrump/status/1080457560291987457.

29. Daniel Dale (@ddale8), tweet, October 23, 2019, https://twitter.com /ddale8/status/1187111478547177473.

AFTERWORD: CLOSING THOUGHTS

1. Victims of Communism Memorial Foundation, "US Attitudes Toward Socialism, Communism, and Collectivism," YouGov, October

2019, https://drive.google.com/file/d/1-Finnggps7JDvgoylYYWc_on PtP8UiR8/view.

2. "Executive Order 9066: Resulting in the Relocation of Japanese (1942)," February 19, 1942, National Archives, https://www.ourdocu ments.gov/doc.php?flash=false&doc=74#.

3. Thom Tillis, "I Support Trump's Vision on Border Security. But I Would Vote Against the Emergency," *Washington Post*, February 25, 2019, https://www.washingtonpost.com/opinions/2019/02 /25/i-support-trumps-vision-border-security-i-would-vote-against -emergency/.

4. Ibid.

5. Scott Wong and Alexander Bolton, "GOP's Tillis Comes Under Pressure for Taking on Trump," *The Hill*, March 13, 2019, https://thehill .com/homenews/senate/433929-gops-tillis-comes-under-pressure-for -taking-on-trump.

6. Brian Murphy, "Tillis Reverses Course, Votes to Support Trump on National Emergency Declaration," *News & Observer* [Raleigh, NC], March 14, 2019, https://www.newsobserver.com/news/politics-gov ernment/article227742754.html.

7. Gary D. Robertson, "Rep. Mark Walker Declines Tillis Primary Challenge," *News & Record* [Greensboro, NC], June 13, 2019, https:// www.greensboro.com/news/state/rep-mark-walker-declines-tillis -primary-challenge/article_10e7e0c1-ec31-5265-9857-baf0b43a756e .html.

8. Gary D. Robertson, "Trump Endorses North Carolina Sen. Thom Tillis," Associated Press, June 25, 2019, https://apnews.com /3bf80ecb6a6a42f58a640e2b4e669ca8.

About the Author

JOE WALSH is a former Illinois congressman elected to Congress in the Tea Party wave of 2010. Following his service in Congress, Walsh became one of the most popular conservative talk radio hosts in the country, syndicated in major markets throughout the U.S.